A WORK IN PROGRESS

A WORK IN PROGRESS

Embracing the Life God Gave You

JULIA MARIE HOGAN WERNER, LCPC

Our Sunday Visitor
Huntington, Indiana

Our Sunday Visitor Publishing Division
Our Sunday Visitor, Inc.
200 Noll Plaza
Huntington, IN 46750
www.osv.com
1-800-348-2440

ISBN: 978-1-68192-634-6 (Inventory No. T2495)
1. SELF-HELP—Personal Growth—Happiness.
2. SELF-HELP—Personal Growth—General.
3. RELIGION—Christianity—Catholic.

eISBN: 978-1-68192-635-3
LCCN: 2021952972

Cover and interior design: Lindsey Riesen
Cover art: Adobe Stock

PRINTED IN THE UNITED STATES OF AMERICA

For Johnny.
There's no one I'd rather be on this journey with.

Contents

Contents

Introduction

D oes it ever seem like life just happens to you? Do you get that feeling that everyone else around you knows the script, and you're left in the dark, trying to catch up? How does everyone else seem to be so sure about their life's purpose? What is the secret to being confident about living your life and making good things happen?

We are all looking for purpose and engaging, meaningful experiences in life, especially as young adults. When that purpose isn't immediately apparent, we feel adrift and unsure. We're tempted to take a passive approach to life and just hope it will all work out. The result is that we feel anxious, directionless, and unsure of what to do with ourselves. Many of us waste precious time and energy pursuing and following the wrong purpose. In fact, young adults today (whether you are Generation Z or a Millennial) report that they feel uncertain about the future.[1] They also report increased levels of anxiety and depression due to the pressures of

---

[1] https://www2.deloitte.com/global/en/pages/about-deloitte/articles/millennialsurvey.html

life and their sense of lacking connection.[2]

Consider the following questions:

- Does not knowing where your life is headed cause you anxiety?
- What would a meaningful and authentic life look like for you?
- What steps would you need to take, or what skills would you need to learn, to create that life for yourself?
- What role does God play in your plan for your life?
- Do you have a sense of what God is asking you to do with your life?

If you feel uncertain about your answer to any of these questions, you are not alone. I wrote this book because we've all asked ourselves these questions in some form at different points in our lives. Sometimes the answers are clear; often they are not. A Deloitte study found that Millennials are looking for a purposeful life that includes "creating, sharing, and capturing memories earned through experiences that span the spectrum of life's opportunities."[3] The challenge is figuring out how to make that "creating, sharing, and capturing memories" a concrete reality. Many adults in their twenties and thirties feel like they have lost the script to their lives — if they ever had a script in the first place. They feel directionless, unsure, confused, and never really prepared for whatever is going to happen next.

The buzzword "adulting" emerged a few years ago, attempting to capture young adults' struggle to find purpose. The term often referred to completing tasks associated with adulthood, such as car

[2] https://www.thecut.com/2016/03/for-80-years-young-americans-have-been-getting-more-anxious-and-depressed.html
[3] Deloitte, Millennial Survey

maintenance, home repairs, and bill paying (tasks many of us never encountered as carefree kids). But there is so much more to our adult life than creating a budget or completing household chores. It's not so much *what* you do with your life but *how* you do it. If you know your purpose in life, you will live in a radically different way than if you don't know it. And this sense of purpose will certainly impact how you perform basic life tasks, including paying your bills.

Yet the reality is that, as adults, we often find that our childhood dreams have been consigned to daily realities (and realities about ourselves and our limits that we may still struggle to accept). The plans we had for ourselves aren't working out the way we thought they would. We look around and wonder how we missed out on the secret to being successful, happy, and fulfilled in life while others (or everyone!) around us seem to succeed. Were you sick the day they covered this at school? Is there some best-selling book that you haven't read yet? What does everyone else know about "doing life" that you don't?

Think back to your childhood for a moment. What did you want to be when you grew up? Maybe you wanted to be a superhero, a detective, or perhaps the president of the United States. At different points of my childhood, I wanted to be a veterinarian, an architect, an astronaut, and a fiction writer. Yet as I discovered (and as most of us find as we grow up), the hopes and dreams we have for ourselves often change or pan out differently than we expect. Sometimes that's for the better, and sometimes it can be incredibly disappointing. And for many of us, as we seek to make sense of where our lives have ended up, we find ourselves confused, battling uncertainty, stress, and disappointment. Yet we still have to go about the business of being adults. Even if you are content with your current situation, you might find yourself thinking, "Is this really it?" Or perhaps you just feel like something is missing.

I once had a client, Jessica,[4] who came to my office hoping to find a sense of direction and purpose in her life. "I feel so stuck," she told me. "It's like I have all of these things I want to accomplish both in my career and in my personal life, but I just can't seem to do them. Time goes by so fast, and I never seem to be able to start working toward my goals. I feel like everyone else is looking at me thinking, 'She's such a failure.' And I feel like a failure." She felt hopeless, unmotivated, and bombarded by self-critical thoughts (all of which are possible symptoms of depression). Her sense of disconnect between her lived experience and her expectations for her life were affecting her mood and ability to function on a daily basis.

Jessica isn't alone in feeling this way. Many of us place extreme pressure on ourselves to be successful, in whatever way we define "success," and to have it all figured out. Perhaps unsurprisingly, the American Psychological Association found that today's young adults have increased expectations of themselves and others.[5] They view achieving these expectations as a sign of personal success and worth. Conversely, if they fail to meet these expectations, they believe they have failed. The trouble is, many young adults today have unrealistic expectations about life. As a result, they end up setting themselves up for constant disappointment and frustration.

What do I mean about unrealistic expectations? Well, we demand nothing less than perfection from ourselves, and we expect others to live up to the same standards. We want to be the perfect employee, the perfect friend, the perfect partner or spouse — and we expect our coworkers, friends, and significant others to measure up to the same impossible standards. We tend to look on anything other than perfection as a failure, and there is no in-between. And the fear of being anything less than perfect is paralyzing, making it terrifying to even start on any project or venture. Of course, aim-

---

[4] Names and details about clients have been changed throughout. Client examples are a combination of many client experiences and any identifying information has been removed and/or changed.
[5] https://www.apa.org/pubs/journals/releases/bul-bul0000138.pdf

ing to better ourselves is important, but when perfectionism takes over, our goals can create a vacuum that sucks fulfillment and joy out of life.

To further complicate matters, Millennials are putting off traditional milestones like marriage, having children, and buying a house, according to the Pew Research Center.[6] These things have traditionally served as markers of accomplishment. Many young adults now have to postpone these cultural benchmarks for very legitimate reasons, especially financial reasons. Yet because we've always told ourselves that we need to be married by a certain age, have that promotion by a certain age, or basically have life figured out by the time we're thirty, we feel discouraged and disappointed when things don't work out as we planned. When these traditional benchmarks seem just out of reach, it's easy to feel overwhelmed and disappointed instead of confident and ready to move forward with our lives.

As Catholic young adults, we face the additional pressure to discern our vocation. For those who feel called to marriage, when it takes longer than we expected to get married, we feel directionless and confused. This can also come into play if young couples experience fertility issues or other factors that affect their ability to have children. It can be all too easy to fall into the comparison trap, looking at other people's lives and assuming we're doing something wrong because our life doesn't look like theirs.

If this sounds like you, be encouraged: You are not alone. Many young adults today feel like they are being crushed under the weight of external and internal expectations, and they feel overwhelmed and unsure of what direction their life is going to take. And that can be a scary place to find yourself. But that isn't the end of the story.

If you've picked up this book, you know that there is definitely

---

[6] https://www.pewresearch.org/social-trends/2020/05/27/as-millennials-near-40-theyre-approaching-family-life-differently-than-previous-generations/

something more to your life. You might not be quite sure what that "something more" is, but you know it's out there. In this book, we'll explore how to find your personal, God-given purpose and how to find joy in your life, even when it doesn't turn out the way you expect it to. We'll also explore practical strategies to help you live out your purpose on a daily basis. You don't have to have all the answers — in fact, it's not really possible. But I'm here to tell you that it's OK to not have everything figured out. It's absolutely OK. Why? Because we are all on a journey of self-discovery. We are called to be constantly evaluating our lives, shedding what holds us back from being our authentic selves, and embracing what brings us closer to God and our true purpose. We are all a work in progress.

Instead of living reactively, feeling like you are perpetually late to the game, you can take an active role in shaping the trajectory of the life God has given to you — and you can do this without figuring it all out first. It's not an overnight process or step-by-step program; rather, it involves cultivating certain perspectives and attitudes that will allow you to stay open to the invitations God places in your path as you live life. It is a gradual, lifelong process of discernment and collaboration with God.

Let me share an example with you from my own life. Clients, friends, and even people I'm meeting for the first time often ask, "How did you know that you wanted to be a therapist?" I think they are expecting me to say it's what I always wanted, or to talk about the light bulb moment where I said, "Aha! Now I know that I was born to be a therapist."

In reality, my story is far less exciting. In fact, right up until my final year of graduate school, I waffled between wanting to be a therapist and finding a job in Human Resources. It wasn't until I started working with psychotherapy clients as an intern that I realized I really wanted to be — and could be — a therapist.

We are all searching for our personal path in life, whether we use the word "purpose" or not. Of course, we all have an ultimate purpose: to get to Heaven and live in communion with God. The choices we make in our lives bring us closer to this goal or pull us farther away. Much of life is recalibrating, over and over again, as we try to eliminate or mitigate those things that hold us back from our ultimate purpose and spend more time focusing on the things that bring us closer to it.

But there's also the unique way in which we are personally called to pursue our ultimate purpose. Some use the term *vocation* to describe this, but we'll primarily be using the term *purpose* in this book. You've been given a specific set of talents, gifts, and personality characteristics that you are called to use to help you and those you encounter grow closer to God; activating those gifts is your unique purpose in life, your personal path to Heaven.

Identifying your unique purpose is a whole other ball game. Many of us assume that everyone else received a sign from the heavens about their purpose in life, and that we are the odd ones out with no clear direction. Yet this is far from true. In fact, most of us, even those who seem to have everything figured out, occasionally experience that "What am I doing here?" feeling. We all feel a bit lost at times, unsure where our purpose lies, and paralyzed by this uncertainty. I would argue that this is just part of being human. It's knowing how to handle this uncertainty that makes the difference.

It doesn't help that we've lost our sense of purpose and self-knowledge as a culture. Our society tells us that we'll find these things in the right job, the right relationship, the right house, the right amount of money, or the right level or prestige. Even if we reject what the culture offers us, we don't know how to go about finding our purpose. As Catholics, we believe that knowing and loving God is our purpose and that Jesus provides us direction. But what does that actually look like in our day-to-day lives? Without the right tools, it can feel like fumbling for a door handle in complete darkness. That's not a very peaceful or joyful way to find purpose in life. In fact, it can be very anxiety-inducing.

The good news is that you get to take an active role in identifying your purpose and direction in life. In fact, what I propose in this book is that having the courage to participate in God's plan for your life opens up a world of exciting possibilities. This book will offer you a different way to look at life and your unique purpose. You'll see how making decisions, whether big or small, doesn't have to be a stressful and anxiety-inducing process. You'll learn to look beyond the checklist approach to fulfillment, and instead focus on learning more about who you are (self-knowledge) to guide you in finding purpose and making decisions in life. When you know who you are and your purpose, it's so much easier to trust yourself to make decisions. You'll find that letting go of your expectations about what you "should" do will free you to make choices and to live your daily life with confidence and a sense of purpose.

You see, we are so much more than our jobs, our relationships, where we live, how much money we make, or what kind of car we drive. But when we get wrapped up in the checklist of life, looking to it to provide our sense of purpose, we forget where our true worth lies. We forget that our identity is rooted in the fact that God loved us into existence and continues to love us unconditionally, regardless of how we are doing in life. God's love for us isn't dependent on what we do; it is dependent on who we are: loved by God. This is the most important definition of our identity and should be the foundation for everything else. We are created and loved by God. If we don't understand our purpose in light of this reality, then we won't be able to see ourselves as we really are, and we will struggle to find happiness and peace in our relationships with others and even with ourselves.

Over the course of this book, we'll take a look at seven habits that cause us to lose sight of our identity and purpose:

- Living life according to external expectations
- Failing to identify priorities (or having the wrong priorities)

- Letting things happen rather than making decisions
- Not establishing boundaries in relationships
- Ignoring authentic self-care
- Refusing to acknowledge our limits
- Being afraid to make a commitment

We'll also explore seven practices that can help you regain your sense of self and purpose:

- Letting go of arbitrary expectations
- Identifying your priorities
- Making decisions confidently
- Establishing boundaries
- Practicing self-care
- Acknowledging your limits
- Embracing commitment

These seven practices will help you develop a sense of authentic purpose. They will help free you to weather any season of life, whether calm or storm, with peace because you will know who you are. And even the most difficult moments won't be able to rob you of that peace.

Each chapter contains reflection questions for personal journaling to help you explore the concepts covered, and in the appendix you'll find discussion questions for group work. Each chapter also includes action items to help you implement the specific ideas and suggestions.

You don't have to feel like you are out of control and white-knuckling through life. You can experience a peaceful sense of purpose and confidence in yourself.

Let's get started!

1

Who Are You?

"Who are you?"
What comes to mind when you hear that question? How do you respond? Does it make you feel uncomfortable? When I ask my psychotherapy clients this question, many of them laugh nervously, squirm in their seats, and struggle to come up with an answer. And to be honest, I think it would take me a minute or two to figure out how to answer it myself. Even though it can be an uncomfortable question when I ask it, it gives me an invaluable sense of how my clients view themselves — their strengths, weaknesses, self-knowledge, and other insights. This is important because knowing who you are is a critical step in your development as a person.

Psychologist Erik Erikson (1902–1994) developed a famous system of human development that is divided into eight stages. The fifth critical stage is development of one's identity; the sixth is development of intimacy with others (not just romantic relationships). In other words, knowing who you are provides a foundation upon which you can establish authentic relationships with others and make choices in line with your values and purpose in life. What happens when you can't create a strong sense of identity and connection with others? According to Erikson, the result is role confusion and isolation. When you aren't clear and confident about who you are, your relationships with others are more likely to be based on surface-level or inauthentic connections rather than authentic ones.

Unfortunately, there is a great deal of noise — from our culture, ourselves, and others — surrounding the question "Who are you?" The reality is that for all of us, this question can tap into our deepest insecurities.

Even if it makes you uncomfortable, it's important to consider this question for yourself. The way you answer it (and even the struggles you face in trying to answer it) can reveal what story you are telling yourself about your life. While your story might not feature you being thrust into the spotlight to save the world before a giant meteor hits the earth, like the latest summer blockbuster, your life is a story, and it is a valuable one. It's a story that matters, and how you tell this story matters, because it can shine a light on how you view yourself and your purpose. And when you begin to tell your story, you give yourself the chance to embrace your current narrative or, if necessary, rewrite it.

Here are some common stories that need to be evaluated and rewritten. These are examples I often encounter in my work with my clients, and I know they're fairly common in our society:

- "I've never really fit in anywhere, and I often feel lonely because I don't have many friends."
- "No one in my life understands me."
- "I never feel like I am enough. I try to do everything 'right,' and yet I never feel like I can earn love and ap-

proval from people in my life."
- "Nothing seems to work in my favor."
- "I try to be nice and generous toward others, but they never seem to reciprocate and instead I feel resentful and emotionally drained."
- "I just pretend to be happy and bubbly so that others won't see my imperfections."
- "I feel like I am constantly trying to be perfect but am forever failing at it. My story is one of failure."
- "I get excited about projects, start them, and then quickly lose steam. My life feels like a bunch of unfinished projects."
- "There's nothing wrong with me. It's everyone else who doesn't have it together."
- "I'm too lazy/impatient/imperfect/sinful to be a good person."

Do you hear yourself in any of these stories? In what ways is your story different? How is it the same? Notice that a common thread through all of these stories is the focus on what's wrong: feeling lonely, inadequate, taken for granted, unlovable, imperfect, unfinished, stuck, or limited. When our identity is clouded by these feelings of inadequacy and loneliness, we end up telling false stories about ourselves and believing they're the truth of who we are. These stories become what I call *false friends*: those standards by which we measure our identity and feel as if they are true, but which actually erode our true sense of self. These false friends knock us off-center and distract us from our true purpose instead of bringing us closer to it.

How do these false friends become the powerful driving force behind the stories we tell about ourselves? Each of us has a laundry list of our perceived imperfections, the qualities we wish we could change, and the things about us that we are uncomfortable sharing with others. Whether these things are true or not, it can be difficult and painful to acknowledge them, because we believe these qualities define us. Whether we are consciously aware of them or not, they influence what we believe about ourselves and our purpose.

A second likely reason these false friends are so powerful is that when we focus on our imperfections, whether real or imagined, we neglect to stop and reflect on the most authentic source of our identity and worth. The truth is that our imperfections, limitations, and less desirable qualities don't define who we really are. Set aside the laundry list of your flaws for a moment and focus on the simple but profound fact that you are created in love by God, in his image and likeness, called to be his son or daughter. Pause for a moment and think about the impact of this truth and what it means about your identity and worth. Before you were born, God knew and loved you. And the very fact that you exist means that you are loved by God. This has nothing to do with where you are in life. Another way of saying it: Because God loves you, you exist. You matter. God wanted you to exist, and so you were loved into existence. It's that simple.

We rarely pause to consider how radical this simple reality is, but we desperately need to do just that. Yes, we probably learned this in religion class growing up, but we too easily forget the profound impact this fundamental truth has for us in the midst of our day-to-day lives and stresses.

In my living room, I keep a framed print of a quote that reads:

> Have patience with all things but first with yourself.
> Never confuse your mistakes with your value as a human being.
> You are a perfectly valuable, creative, worthwhile person simply because you exist.
> And no amount of triumphs or tribulations can ever change that.

This quote perfectly sums up the profound origin of our worth. Our endless quest to prove we are "enough" is unnecessary. Our worth and identity have already been given to us by God, and we have nothing more to prove.

Venerable Julia Greeley[7] exemplified how this knowledge of our true worth can inform our seemingly ordinary, everyday lives. Julia was born as an enslaved person in Missouri. One of her eyes was permanently injured by a whip when she was five years old. After the Civil War, she worked in Colorado, cleaning houses and churches and doing laundry. She also provided child care for families in the area. She is best known for her love of the poor. She was known to drop off needed items to poor families in the middle of the night because she knew many of them were embarrassed to accept help. It was only at her funeral, where hundreds of people came to pay their respects, that the true impact this "Angel of Charity" had on the poor, the firemen, and others was recognized.

Julia lived a hard life and encountered great cruelty, yet she chose to live a life of love, generosity, and service, with little thanks or recognition. To be able to live her life in this way, she needed to be convicted of her worth and identity as beloved by God. Certainly she did not receive that validation from many in her life, especially in her early years, yet she knew her purpose and she lived it out to the best of her ability.

So I'll ask again: Who are you?

You are not the sum of your accomplishments, nor are you defined by your good or bad deeds. Instead, you are a person who is worthy of love simply because you exist. Far from being a cliché, this is the very foundation of the story of your life.

Yet too often, the knowledge that we are created in the image and likeness of God and loved by our Creator as we are, right now, often takes a backseat to those false friends mentioned above. They

---

[7] https://coloradosun.com/2018/08/09/julia-greeley-denver-sainthood-process/

cloud our vision, making it very challenging at times to remember who we really are. This can leave us feeling like we've been set adrift in life, rather than having a clear sense of direction. These false friends are distractions that pull us away from living our life rooted in our true identity. And when this happens, our false friends become the primary drivers behind our decision-making.

This is why so often we make decisions out of fear instead of confidence and conviction, and it leads us to one of two places: Either we give up and take a completely passive attitude toward life, or we become consumed by the need to try to control everything. Taking a passive approach to life means we just sit back and wait for things to happen. When we take a controlling approach toward life, we try to force everything to fit with our view of perfection — and when things don't go our way, we think it's all over. We may even wonder where God is in our life and assume that it's up to us to make things turn out well for us. Neither of these extremes make it easy to live life based on our true identity and purpose.

Thankfully, you can steer clear of both of these extremes. Identifying the false friends that have hijacked the story of your life empowers you to let them go, so that you can embrace your authentic self. Your goal is to remove the roadblocks that are preventing you from being authentically you in every area of your life. While this process may sound complex and intimidating at first, it isn't as uncomfortable or as overwhelming as you might think. In fact, discovering who you really are can actually be an exciting and freeing process. I've witnessed the positive transformations many of my clients have made as they cleared away their own personal roadblocks — whether they are coping with the loss of someone or something in their life, discerning a career path, healing from trauma, or growing in their own sense of self-worth and confidence. In my own life, I've witnessed the freedom that can come from letting go of using productivity and "doing things" as a measurement of my worth.

Over the next several chapters, we will take a look at six common roadblocks you might face in seeking to identify and embrace your true self, as well as practical ways to address them. They are:

1. Living your life according to unrealistic expectations. (Spoiler alert: Expecting yourself to be perfect every waking moment is unrealistic.)
2. Failing to identify or clearly define your priorities, or clinging to the wrong priorities. (This can be the difference between being confident with where your life is headed or feeling adrift.)
3. Avoiding decisions. (Indecision can be paralyzing!)
4. Neglecting proper self-care. (Sorry, binge-watching your favorite TV show and scrolling through your newsfeed don't count as authentic self-care. We'll talk about that.)
5. Ignoring the reality of your limits. (As much as I wish we could, we can't do it all.)
6. Refusing to make commitments. (Yes, commitment is scary, but it can be incredibly freeing.)

As we dive into these roadblocks over the next several chapters, we'll also discuss how you can begin to clear them away so that you can accept the truth of who you are.

Reflection Questions
- What stories do I tell myself about my life? What are my false friends?
- Do I tend to take a more passive or a more controlling attitude toward life? What is the result?
- What could a balanced life look like for me?

Action Items
- Spend five to ten minutes describing the balanced life

you want to live. Dream big!

- What are the roadblocks that make it difficult for you
to live a more balanced life? (Keep these in mind as
you read future chapters, as we'll likely cover them
there.) After you've written a description of a balanced
life, reflect on what is getting in the way of you being
able to live that life. I'd recommend making it into a
list for reference as you continue to work your way
through the book.

2

Challenging Expectations

K nowing your identity is critical, because it determines the way you approach your life. When you are clear about who you are, it is much easier to discern what you can expect from yourself, others, and your life. On the other hand, when you aren't clear about who you are, you're prone to a lot more confusion. It's easy to expect the wrong things for your life when you haven't taken the time to identify your authentic self. It's also far too easy to let other people set those expectations for you. That's why the first roadblock we need to work through in embracing our true identity is false or unrealistic expectations.

When you think about your plans for the future, what comes to mind? Maybe you want to start a business, have a family, or travel. Or maybe you don't like thinking about the future. Perhaps instead of feeling excited about your plans, you feel dread or anxiety.

What are your expectations for your life? Where do you want to be in five years? Ten years? When do you want to retire? What words are going through your head? Chances are that you hear a lot of "shoulds" as you consider the expectations you have for yourself:

- I should have already started a business.
- I should be ready to start a family.
- I should have enough money saved to travel in the next (fill-in-the-blank) years.
- I should have better grades.
- I should have a better job.
- I should have an easier time with this.
- I should exercise more.
- I should eat healthier.
- I should be in a relationship.
- I should be able to juggle everything.
- I should have the energy to do this.
- I should already know how to do this.
- I should be present to everyone in my life, and it should be easy.
- I should be able to do this without feeling guilty.
- I should have an easier time making friends.
- I should have an easier time staying organized.
- I should be able to be on time.
- I should be able to finish everything on my to-do list.

You get the picture. Our daily thoughts are filled with "should" statements. And we put a lot of pressure on ourselves to meet these expectations. These "shoulds" can start to feel a lot more like demands than dreams, making life feel like it's all about meeting obligations. With so many shoulds in our thought patterns, it's no wonder so many of us constantly feel like we simply can't measure up.

In this chapter, we're going to take a look at the power of the expectations we set for ourselves (those "should" statements). We'll consider how expectations are formed, how to identify them, and how to discern whether they are healthy or unhealthy, realistic or unrealistic. This chapter is your chance to pause and reflect on your own values and expectations, to choose which ones you want to keep, and to choose which ones you want to let go of and replace with better ones. After you've completed this chapter, you'll start seeing how expectations are everywhere!

What Are Expectations?

Expectations are essentially the standards we set for how to behave, what goals we pursue, and assumptions we make about what determines our worth. We apply these expectations to ourselves and to others to help guide the way we understand our purpose and place in the world. It can be helpful to think of expectations as computer programming code, or a script that is automatically run when we encounter a specific situation. And it is important to note that we don't often intentionally choose these scripts. Instead, they form subconsciously and are based on our life experience, relationships, and feedback from others. These expectations can be helpful or hurtful — but more on this later.

   We live our lives and make decisions based on our own expectations and those of others. First, there are our own expectations. We expect things from ourselves and from others. All of us have scripts for both ourselves and for those around us, which result from our beliefs about our own worth and the worth we place on others. These scripts are based on what we think we "should" achieve, how we think we "should" treat others, and how we believe we "should" be treated by others. In other words, we expect ourselves and others to act in certain ways. For example, "I should be able to juggle my overfilled schedule without getting stressed." Or, "If they really cared about me, they would know I am hurt without me having to tell them how I am feeling."

   Second, there are expectations that others have of us. It's important to note that we cannot get inside other people's heads, but we easily forget this fact and believe that we are, in fact, mind readers. Very often, we think we know other people's expectations and live our life and make decisions based on what we think we know, forgetting to investigate their validity first. Many of us believe that our families and friends will only accept or love us if we "prove" our worth, perhaps by succeeding or being the "best" at everything, or perhaps by always being available to them no matter what. We may have similar assumptions about our coworkers' expectations, or even those of complete strangers.

Sometimes other people communicate their expectations to us, such as our parents expecting us to be home by a certain time every night when we were teens. And there are also expectations we understand implicitly, even if they are never communicated. For example, perhaps your friend group has an unspoken expectation that you don't date a friend's ex even if that's never been explicitly discussed. Another example could be the gender role expectations in a relationship. Both partners might have unspoken expectations regarding who does which chores, and so on. Again, it is important to reiterate that not all expectations are bad. Some are actually helpful! But some are not so helpful, and it is our task to discern which is which.

Whether from ourselves or from others, real or perceived, expectations influence many areas of our lives, from how we relate to ourselves, to how we relate to others, to the decisions that we make.

Where Do Expectations Come From?

Our expectations for ourselves and others are shaped first by our childhood experiences. When we were young, our brains were like sponges, and we soaked up what we observed in the world around us. Through our observations, we learned about many things, including communication, relationships, manners, problem-solving, and play. We learned from our primary caregivers (for most of us, these were our parents) how we "should" act, think, and feel. These expectations come with us into adulthood, and they might be healthy or unhealthy, depending on a number of factors: personality, childhood experiences, trauma, and our parents' parenting style, among other things.

For example, one boy's parents might have told him, "Be a big boy and stop crying," and so he learned that he must hide any negative emotions because they were not welcome in his family. This expectation may have then been reinforced by society telling him that "real men don't cry" or "adults have to be strong and not show emotion." Another boy might have heard, "It's OK to be sad. Here are some ways to help you feel better when you're sad." This boy learned that it's fine to express emotions, and he learned healthy ways of doing so. These are two very different expectations regarding emotions. Think about it for a moment: What were the expectations around emotions in your own family?

As we got older, our peers also influenced our expectations, either reinforcing or shifting the expectations we learned at home. A young woman might have learned that she was accepted and welcomed by her peers when she was funny and upbeat, and so she adopted the expectation, "I make and keep friends by being 'the funny one,' but if I show my emotional or deeper side, I won't be accepted." She learned to keep her deeper thoughts to herself and stuck to being the class clown. This is a negative example, but our peers can also help us form healthy and realistic expectations. Friends can also teach us to expect that our friends will be dependable and accept us for who we are. Healthy friendships can also teach us the value of perseverance and dedication. The point is that our life experiences and interactions with others shape not only our values but also the expectations we adopt as guidelines for the way we live our lives and interact with others.

Societal shifts also contribute to the expectations we set (or don't set) for ourselves. A 2017 study from the American Psychological Association (APA) found that younger generations of adults have higher expectations for themselves and others than do older generations.[8] But it's interesting to note what those expectations are: 81 percent of Americans born in the 1980s identified becoming materially rich as an important life goal. This is 20 percent higher than those born in the 1960s. While there are many factors involved, our society has put an increased emphasis on material wealth as a sign of success, worth, and value. This creates the expectation that our value is based on the amount of money we make. Of course, it's easy to see how that takes our focus from what really determines our worth (being daughters and sons of God) and places it on something arbitrary and ever-changing.

It's true that the majority of us don't sit down, take out a notebook and pen, and make a list of all the expectations we have for ourselves and other people. The actual way we form expectations is much more unconscious and subtle. In fact, our expectations are often formed without us being consciously aware of the process. Psychotherapy can be very helpful in uncovering and revealing those expectations that operate in the background of our lives. These expectations are woven so tightly into the framework with which we see the world that they can be difficult to untangle at first. However, through personal reflection, and therapy if needed, we can slowly begin to untangle our expectations and evaluate them one by one.[9]

Knowing where your various expectations originated is important, as it allows you to figure out how to respond to them. As you begin to understand the implicit and explicit expectations you have for yourself, you can sort through them and decide which are healthy and worth keeping, and which are unhealthy and need to be let go or modified.

---

[8] https://www.apa.org/pubs/journals/releases/bul-bul0000138.pdf
[9] Some of our expectations are so deeply ingrained that we may not be able to see them on our own. Therapy can be a very helpful process to help us discern our unhealthy expectations and begin to let them go.

To help you identify some of your expectations, it may be helpful to ask yourself the following questions:

- Where does the word "should" often come up for me?
- When I think about what success means to me, what comes to mind?
- What expectations did my family communicate to me about emotions, relationships, conflict, success, work, worth, and so on?
- What areas of my life do I give myself a hard time about? (e.g., body image, job status, grades, relationship status, etc.)
- What factors routinely affect my self-esteem and self-confidence in a negative way?
- When I think of someone I admire in my life, do I feel motivated and inspired by them or discouraged by their accomplishments?
- What do I wish I could change about my life? What do these things tell me about the expectations I have for myself?

Values and Expectations

In order to shine light on your expectations, it's also helpful to pause and look at your values. Values are the things that are most important to us. Values also signify to us — and this is very important to note — what qualities we use to measure our own worth and the worth of others. If you value financial success, you are likely to measure your worth and the worth of others by this attribute. If you value romantic relationships, you might judge yourself harshly for not being in one, or you may compromise your ideals in order to maintain an unhealthy relationship.

Our values are often shaped by our childhood experiences, our family of origin, our peers, and those we look up to, like mentors, coaches, athletes, and celebrities. Keep in mind that our values can be either helpful or unhelpful. Perhaps you learned growing up that your family supported one another through thick and thin. As an adult, you value family as a place of support, no matter what happens. This is a helpful value. But perhaps you learned through your childhood experiences that you will receive love and attention only when you perform well. As an adult, you may value the feeling that you are doing what must be done to earn love and attention. This is an unhelpful value.

As you consider your values, think about where they came from and how they have played out in your life. How did your early childhood experiences shape your values? Do you have any specific memories of the way these values played out in day-to-day life in your family? Did they help you feel more authentically "you," or did they leave you feeling less authentic?

Because values tend to be more abstract — we value things like perfection, success, and the "perfect" and "ideal" family and relationships — they are easier to understand by considering the ways in which we live them out. Our expectations are the lived experience of our values. Our values set the direction for our actions, while our expectations are the manifestations of our values. Think about the value of financial success. An expectation based on this value might be that we must choose the highest paying job, even if that means passing over a more fulfilling one. It might look like choosing our friends based on their financial success. Or it could look like judging ourselves or others harshly because we don't make "enough" money.

An expectation based on valuing relationships might be that we have to find a partner. As a result, we put pressure on ourselves to find someone, or perhaps we leap into relationships or speed up the pace of our relationships without incorporating healthy boundaries or a discernment process. Or we might remain in an unhappy relationship for fear of being single. Our expectations help put our values into action, for better or for worse.

There's a cyclical relationship between our values and expectations. They reveal one another. This is important as you work to discern your own values and expectations. You can either consider your values in light of your expectations, or you can identify your expectations first in order to discern your values.

As you begin the process of discerning what to keep and what to toss, keep this in mind: If your values are good and healthy, chances are your expectations will also be good and healthy. On the other hand, if a value is unhealthy, you will also want to address the expectations that are based on that value. It works the same way if you start with your expectations.

As you start to identify your own values, follow these three helpful steps:

1. **Make a list of activities, experiences, work projects, and characteristics (both personal and general) that make you feel alive, that you are excited about, that you look forward to.** Examples: Doing activities with others, creating things, being active, being reflective, learning, and the like. We all have a different combination of things that bring us a sense of excitement and fulfillment.

2. **Identify some common themes you see in the items on this list.** Examples: Community, time alone to recharge, creativity, quality time, connection, collaboration, being present, leading, attention to detail, being authentic, among other traits.

3. **Based on the themes you've identified, identify two or three words that summarize these themes. These are your values.** Examples: Presence, authenticity, community. These keywords can help to summarize your personal values and provide a framework for you

to incorporate them into both your daily life and your overall life path.

Toxic Expectations

On the surface, having expectations for how you live your life and how others should act sounds helpful. After all, shouldn't we have standards? Of course we should, but they need to be realistic and healthy, grounded in an authentic understanding of our true selves. The trouble is, many of our expectations are founded on unchallenged and arbitrary assumptions of what we think we "should" do.

A good place to start with discerning whether or not your expectations are realistic and helpful is to first take a look at the expectations you have for yourself. These are the primary driving force behind many of the decisions we make for ourselves. For example, if you have an expectation for yourself that you must always be the best at everything you do, that will shape how much time, attention, and energy you put into obligations in your life. In some ways, this can be helpful. Having motivation to get things done well is a good thing, after all! But it can also be harmful, especially when you push yourself too hard, at the expense of your mental and physical health, or even your relationships.

We must take the time to untangle our expectations in order to discern whether they are healthy or unhealthy, realistic or unrealistic. A general rule of thumb is that unhealthy and unrealistic expectations tend to be strict, rigid, and difficult or impossible to achieve. They leave us feeling discouraged and unmotivated. In fact, research has shown that rigid and inflexible thinking patterns can worsen symptoms of depression[10] and are linked to other forms of emotional distress.[11] When the expectations we have for ourselves are inflexible, we can get stuck, missing opportunities for growth and grace.

When your expectations cause you to feel discouraged, take a

---

[10] https://link.springer.com/article/10.1007/s12144-019-00450-3

[11] https://psychcentral.com/lib/rigidity-versus-flexibility-the-key-to-mental-health

step back and ask yourself these questions:

- What is my expectation here?
- Where is this expectation coming from?
- Is this expectation realistic?
- Does this expectation trap me into black-and-white, all-or-nothing thinking?
- Does this expectation fit with who I believe I am called to be?

I can think of a simple example from my own life that shows how unexamined expectations can be unhealthy. I enjoy running a few times a week for exercise and as a stress-reliever. About two years ago, I noticed that I had developed intense heel and knee pain after my runs. At first, the pain would last for a few hours and then go away, but it got to the point where it never seemed to fully disappear between running days. I finally decided to schedule an appointment with my chiropractor, and after several (painful) sessions, he was able to put everything back in alignment. I could run pain-free again! But here's where my unexamined expectations got in the way: I expected that once I could run without pain, and if I made sure to stretch after each run, everything in my body would stay in alignment and I wouldn't need to continue to stretch properly and be mindful of the issues that caused that pain in the first place. So when the pain returned, I felt discouraged, and I was frustrated that I kept having to go back to the chiropractor and take the extra time to stretch. After a few months of feeling disappointed and frustrated, I finally asked my chiropractor if I would ever fully heal. He explained, "Our bodies need regular maintenance, even professional athletes whose job it is to be healthy. Just like a car or anything mechanical, after repeated use, things can get out of alignment from daily wear and tear." I needed to change my expectations so that I could see future appointments and the extra time

I needed to spend stretching as positive investments in my health. This helped me identify an unhealthy and unexamined expectation in myself about what healing really meant.

If we never question our expectations, we end up letting false expectations drive us, which has a toxic effect on our emotional, mental, physical, relational, and spiritual well-being. For many of us, our guiding expectation in life is really an impossible standard of perfection. This is called perfectionism, and it's a serious problem. Perfectionism can show up in all sorts of little ways in our lives. In my work as a psychotherapist, I regularly encounter clients who are beating themselves up for things like sending an email with a typo, not responding with more empathy to a friend, or forgetting an appointment. We've programmed ourselves to expect perfection and nothing less, and we believe that good people never make mistakes. This is simply not true.

Perfectionism can also show up in bigger ways in our lives, coloring our expectations of what it means to be a "good" employee, boss, friend, partner, daughter, son, sibling, or parent. When we don't live up to these expectations — whatever they might be — we feel like a failure, and we sink deeper into the rut of beating ourselves up. Perfectionism becomes an ongoing cycle of setting ourselves up for failure and then punishing ourselves for failing, over and over again.

If you want a clear example of how toxic our unhealthy expectations can be, consider society's ideal of the "perfect" body type, for both men and women. For far too long, the fashion industry has presented us with a completely unrealistic standard of beauty: for women, it is tall with a small waist, large hips and chest, and long legs (and often Caucasian). For men, it is tall, extremely muscular, and again, often Caucasian. Yet while these body types have been touted as ideal, the images we see in advertisements are completely unattainable; often, even the supposedly "perfect" models have been digitally altered. These images don't exist in the physical world. Yet because this is the standard of perfection, we all struggle with feelings of inadequacy because we don't have the "perfect" body type. Fortunately, there has recently been a shift in the advertising and fashion industries, and many stores and magazines have begun to embrace a "no Photoshop" policy, using models that represent a range of body types and ethnicities. These changes in the industry are helping to shift the expectations we have for our bodies — but there is still a long way to go.

Even if you haven't personally been affected by the culture's views on body image, you can probably think of other ways that social media and the advertising industry have shaped your expectations of yourself and others. These experiences show how we can form expectations without being aware that we are forming them.

How to Let Go of Expectations

Summer, a client of mine, was in her mid-twenties. She sought out therapy for her depression and sense of a general lack of direction in her life. She had attended a prestigious college and graduated with a degree in biology, but she felt like her life had stalled after graduation. She was working part-time at a clothing store, despite her ultimate goal of working at the local zoo, and she felt stuck in her life in many ways. She knew that she could start applying for internships and entry-level positions at the zoo, or that she could seek out work as a veterinary technician to get some experience in the field, but she struggled to even log onto job posting sites to see what was available. She felt guilt — "My parents are so frustrated with me because I'm not even using my degree" — and shame — "I'm such a failure because I can't even get myself to click a few buttons to submit my resume" — because of her struggles. Through our work together, Summer was able to begin to let go of the expectation that she should have everything in her life figured out and lined up. Over time, she was able to become more and more comfortable with not having everything figured out. She slowly began to focus on the present and what was best for her, instead of allowing what she "should" do to overwhelm her. Once Summer freed herself from the pressure of arbitrary expectations, she felt more free to live her life with confidence, even though she hadn't found her dream job quite yet.

On the surface, Stacey's life couldn't have looked more different than Summer's. Stacey was in her sixties and had been working at the same company for over thirty years. She and her husband were empty nesters. She enjoyed her job and was proud of her work, but lately she noticed that she was feeling dissatisfied. She wondered whether she had lived a meaningful life and questioned some of her past decisions. She felt stagnant and wanted to make some changes to feel a sense of fulfillment again. Through our work together, Stacey was able to identify the expectations that were making her unhappy. She had pictured traveling the world with her husband, spoiling her grandchildren, and volunteering for several nonprofits. Instead, she was still working and hadn't taken any big trips with her husband for several years. She didn't have any grandchildren, and her work schedule made it challenging to commit to a consistent volunteer schedule. Stacey realized that the trouble wasn't her lifestyle. The trouble was that she had expectations about what things made for a meaningful life, and those things were absent from her life. Over time, Stacey was able to replace her expectations with realistic alternatives that freed her to find meaning in her actual circumstances.

Both Summer and Stacey found freedom and satisfaction once they learned to let go of their limiting expectations and were free to see the possibilities in the present. In a similar way, once you've identified the expectations you've set for yourself, you can decide whether they help you be more authentically you in the way that God has called you to be. Then you can decide which expectations to keep and which to replace. Let's take a look at some specific ways you can let go of the unhealthy "shoulds" in your life so that you can be free to live in the reality before you.

Free yourself from "should" language.

If you find yourself using a lot of "should" statements, like "I *should* be further along in my career by now" or "I *should* be able to get everything done on my to-do list without fail," you are falling into the trap of unrealistic expectations. Here's a hint: Expectations that include the word "should" tend to be unrealistic. When you encounter your own "shoulds," take a step back and challenge those statements by reframing them to be more realistic and empowering.

When you think, "I should be further along in my career right now," pause. How can you address this expectation? Perhaps you can remind yourself, "I still have goals I need to achieve, but I am also proud of all I have accomplished so far." This is much more empowering and realistic because it acknowledges your accomplishments, while also opening the way to more goals for the future. Try to catch yourself every time you use a "should" statement and take a moment to consider whether or not it is a realistic expectation.

Learn to recognize all-or-nothing and black-and-white thinking patterns.

As we mentioned earlier, these thinking patterns usually lead to you feeling either like a complete success or an utter failure, with no room for anything in between. If you find yourself becoming angry with yourself (or others) for things you "always" or "never" do, this is a good indicator that you've got an unrealistic expectation. A good way to challenge this expectation is to rephrase the statement in a way that's not so black-and-white. For example, perhaps you catch yourself worrying, "I'll never be in a healthy relationship. It will always end in a breakup." Instead of thinking "never" and "always," consider the reality. You might tell yourself, "One of my goals is to be in a healthy relationship, but I know that I can find joy and fulfillment no matter what my relationship status happens to be. What matters more is that I am pursuing a meaningful life daily." This style of thinking is much more freeing and empowering.

Be wary of perfection.

When we expect perfection of ourselves or others, we pretty much guarantee that we'll feel like a failure. No one is perfect. The good news is, God doesn't expect us to be. Yes, he encourages us to constantly work to be better and to grow in holiness, but even if we're the holiest person on earth, we can still make a mistake. We are human and we fall from time to time. This does not mean we aren't worthwhile. Knowing this, we can pick ourselves up, dust off the dirt, and try again.

For example, let's say that you set a goal of improving your prayer life. It's tempting to say, "Unless I meditate and pray for twenty minutes every day, I am failing at my prayer life." This goal ends up being more discouraging than empowering. What's wrong with wanting to pray for twenty minutes, you ask? Nothing! In fact, this is a good goal. It becomes a problem when we equate our spiritual "success" with praying in a very specific way every day. Not only does this set you up to feel like a failure, but it can block God from leading you into holiness according to his plan. Focusing on how we are failing discourages us from trying again, or reevaluating our goals and how we approach them. Saint Francis de Sales says, "When we aim at perfection, we must aim at the center, but we must not be troubled if we do not always hit it." He also says, "We must not be astonished to see ourselves imperfect, since we must never see ourselves otherwise in this life."[12] Recognizing and living with our imperfections is part of being human — and God knows that we aren't perfect. After all, God created us!

Instead of setting an arbitrary standard of perfection for your prayer life, try focusing on engaging in some form of quality prayer

---

[12] Francis de Sa;les and Henry Benedict Mackey, OSB, *Letters to Persons in Religion* (Eugene, OR; Wipf and Stock Publishers, 2017), 23.

on a daily basis. Ask the Holy Spirit what that prayer should look like, and then follow his inspiration. Reach out to a trusted spiritual director or mentor for this help if you feel stumped about how to proceed. This gives you the freedom to pray in the way that works best for you on any given day, instead of committing yourself to an impossible standard. And when you miss a day, be compassionate toward yourself. Give it to God and plan to begin again tomorrow.

Ask, "Is this moving me toward wholeness, or fostering unease and division in my life?"

Borrowing from Ignatian discernment principles, it is helpful to consider your expectations for yourself in light of these two questions: Are my expectations moving me closer to authenticity and wholeness? Or are they fostering feelings of unease and distance between me and God?

For example, if you find yourself constantly twisting and molding yourself to meet the expectations of others, you are not being your whole self. Instead of discerning how God is inviting you to live your life, which is always with wholeness and authenticity, you are letting yourself be pulled in many different directions in your attempts to meet the expectations of others, which leads to division and inauthenticity.

Embrace self-compassion.

When you find yourself struggling to break the patterns of unhealthy expectations, show yourself some compassion. In practice, this simply means extending the same compassion to yourself that you would show to someone else.

I've done my fair share of double-booking clients or completely forgetting to enter appointments into my calendar. You can imagine my embarrassment when a client shows up anticipating an appointment and I'm completely unprepared. My clients have always graciously forgiven me for my errors. Practicing self-compassion means that I need to be just as compassionate to myself when I make a scheduling error.

If you make a mistake and find yourself thinking, "I never get anything right. I'm such a failure," try replacing that thought with something more compassionate. For instance, "Well, that definitely didn't work out as I had hoped. What can I learn from this experience?" Perhaps you believe that everyone else makes it look so easy, so there must be something wrong with you. Try replacing those thoughts with, "I don't know everyone else's full story. They may be struggling just like me. I can't compare myself to them, because their lives are completely different." Over time, reconsidering your thought patterns can help you be more compassionate toward yourself as you continue on your journey of becoming a more authentic you.

Reflection Questions

- What is one way that society has influenced my expectations of myself? What is one way society has influenced my expectations of others?
- What expectations do I have for myself that are unrealistic or arbitrary? In what ways have these expectations affected me negatively?
- How could my life look different if I were to let go of some of my unrealistic or arbitrary expectations?
- How can I replace my unrealistic and unhealthy expectations with healthy ones?

Action Items

- Identify one expectation you have for yourself that isn't grounded in reality and isn't helping you live an authentic life. Spend some time journaling about why it isn't helping to lead you closer to God and live out your true purpose. Then "make the case" to yourself about why you can and should change your expectation to one that is more helpful.

- Identify one achievable way you can let go of that expectation and the negative impact it is having on your life. Remember, start small!

3

Identifying Your Priorities

So far, we've explored how knowing your true worth and identity as someone created and loved by God forms the foundation for knowing your true purpose in life and how you are called to do good in the world. This truth should inform everything you do! Next we explored how unexamined expectations can keep us stuck and prevent us from really recognizing our true worth. Now we're going to take a deeper look at how identifying your priorities can help you live your life intentionally, rather than feeling like it is getting away from you or that you are wasting your time on things that aren't helping you live out your true purpose. In this chapter, we'll dive into what priorities are and why they are key for actively participating in God's plan for our lives. We will also talk about why having the wrong priorities can make life feel scary, overwhelming, and discouraging. We'll also explore how knowing your values can help you discern your priorities. And finally, we'll explore practical ways to determine your priorities and manage any distractions that might get in the way.

Consider this scenario.

Brian wakes up to the sound of his alarm clock, hits Snooze a few too many times, and then rushes to get ready for the day. He grabs a granola bar, races to work, and walks into a mountain of paperwork and a mile-long to-do list waiting for him at his desk. He has a big project due this week, but he keeps getting interrupted by emails, phone calls, and requests from his coworkers. At the end of the day, he doesn't feel any closer to finishing that big project, and he winds up staying late to try to get some more work done. In the end he just feels tired and frustrated.

Brian has not taken the time to identify his priorities. He finds himself pulled this way and that by whatever feels most urgent in the moment, rather than acting based on clearly set priorities. When our priorities aren't defined, it's easy to feel directionless or behind in life. On the other hand, when we know what our priorities are, we set the tone not only for our day but also for our life. Having carefully chosen priorities empowers us to make decisions that give us a sense of real purpose and lead us closer to God.

If we want to answer the big questions about our lives and our purpose, we first have to take time to evaluate and identify our priorities. We need to examine how we are spending our time and where we are directing our energy. Are we using our energy to achieve those things that are in line with living our life authentically, or are we spending our energy elsewhere? If we don't take the time to examine our priorities, we eventually sap our valuable time and energy, making us unable to focus on the things that really matter.

Why We Need Priorities

Let's take a second look at Brian's story, but this time, let's see what his day could look like with priorities clearly defined.

Brian wakes up to the sound of his alarm clock and allows

himself to hit Snooze once before getting out of bed. He's committed to eating a nutritious breakfast, so he quickly makes himself some eggs and oatmeal. He leaves his house with a five-minute cushion just in case he hits any unexpected traffic on his way to work. When Brian first gets to the office, he grabs some coffee from the break room and then spends the first half hour scanning his inbox and setting his work goals for the day. Because Brian knows he works best with minimal interruptions, and he's got a looming deadline on a big project, he puts on noise-cancelling headphones and takes his laptop to a quiet corner on the office floor. Whenever a new email comes in or a coworker comes by with a request, he makes a note of it on his to-do list and then continues with his current project. At the end of his workday, Brian spends a few minutes sketching out his priorities for tomorrow to ensure a smooth beginning the following day. As he leaves his office, Brian feels content with what he accomplished that day and confident that tomorrow he can pick up right where he left off.

In this second version of the story, Brian chooses where he will direct his time and attention. Notice that he takes the time to make and eat a simple-to-prepare breakfast. He also decides what he wants to work on and how he is going to accomplish it. By simply identifying and honoring those two priorities, he has a much more calm and centered day. Instead of letting his attention and time be dragged to and fro, he decides what is worth his focus. Yes, it takes more planning and a bit more effort, but the results are worth it. When something is important to us, we make it a priority, even if that means being disciplined and intentional.

If we want to shape our everyday lives according to our values, which I define as the "ingredients" of a healthy life, we need to have priorities. Intentionally setting priorities signals to us (and to others) what matters most to us. When something is a true priority, we make time for it. And whether we realize it or not, we will give greater priority to the things we value most. As an example, you might think that working out is a real priority for you, but if you've never been able to establish a healthy workout routine, it's likely that something else is a greater priority. What is it that keeps you from working out? Chances are, you've made that thing a higher priority, whether it should be or not.

Intentionally setting our priorities according to our values promotes balance in life. In the first version of his story, Brian felt like he was being pulled in many different directions and could never seem to focus on what he really wanted to be working on. He felt imbalanced because he hadn't taken the time to identify his priorities. Authentic balance in life is not about having a perfect 50/50 split between work and personal life. Instead, we find authentic balance when we are rooted in our values and living them out on a daily basis, discerning where to direct our time and energy throughout the day.

When we take the time to set our priorities, they become like arrows that point us toward the life God is calling us to live. Living life guided by our priorities frees us to let go of the need to be perfect. Instead, we can begin to seek a life of meaning over a life of perfection. Think of it this way: By honoring our priorities, we are saying "yes" to the fulfilling and authentic life we are meant to live. By contrast, chasing perfection keeps us stuck in the cycle of never feeling good enough because the bar is constantly being raised. Our priorities aren't rules that are meant to be rigidly followed. Instead, they should help us live well even during the most mundane parts of the day (like answering emails, doing paperwork or homework, studying, cleaning, etc.).

So how can we discern which priorities we need to live our life authentically? Self-knowledge is key. Knowing who we are informs the expectations we have for ourselves, and this is the foundation we need to begin to discern our priorities. When our priorities flow from our identity as a son or daughter who is loved by God, it's easier to see what is a mere distraction in our life and what is worth pursuing. Priorities can help us stay on track.

Knowing your values is also important for discerning your priorities. In the last chapter, we defined values as those things that are important to us and that signify how and what an authentic life looks like for us. Knowing your core values helps you set priorities, both for each day and for your life in general. For example, if you value helping others, you can prioritize making sure you do at least one act of kindness for others each day. If you value authentic relationships, you might prioritize connecting with a friend or family member at least once a week. On a broader level, if you value intentionally using the talents God has given you, you might prioritize choosing jobs or projects that allow you to live out that value. Think of your priorities as where you direct your energy based on what your values are. Priorities are the "how," and your values are your "why."

So in order to set your priorities, you need to spend some time thinking about your values. I encourage you to spend some time reflecting on the following questions:

- How do I currently live out my values?
- What values do I want to live out more fully?
- What are some specific ways I can live out my values on a day-to-day basis?
- How can I hold myself accountable for living according to my values? (What priorities can serve as guidelines to keep me on track?)

You might have some similar answers for each of the questions above, and that is OK. All these questions are meant to get you started thinking about what your priorities could look like, and you might keep coming up with the same answers. That's actually a good thing! That likely means that you've zeroed in on a tight set of priorities that are strongly tied to your values. If you have the sense that your list is all over the place, that's OK too. I'd recommend spending some time reflecting on your values and priorities and seeing which ones resonate the most to help you narrow your list down to two or three values and five priorities.

Your list of priorities is meant to be a very practical tool for you to use to guide you throughout each day. It is a checklist of sorts, very different from an examination of conscience. This isn't a checklist about your degree of holiness. Instead, it is a way for you to check in with yourself to determine whether you are spending your time and energy on things that are helping you lead the life you are called to.

When the Wrong Priorities Take Us Off Track

Knowing your values and priorities is one thing, but actually living according to your priorities can be very challenging and even a little messy. Don't let this discourage you. Over time and with practice, you'll get better and better about honoring your values and checking in with yourself to make sure you're living according to your priorities. I don't think I can say this enough when it comes to trying to live authentically: It isn't about being perfect. We can always strive to do better, but we are human beings, which means that we will make mistakes. Not being perfect should never be a reason to feel unworthy or discouraged. Instead, try to view life as a process of learning and improving slowly over time.

One of the primary challenges to living out our values and maintaining focus on our priorities is distractions, whether small or large, internal or external. From the incoming text from a friend to existential questions about ourselves and our limits, distractions pull our gaze away from the meaningful and authentic life we are striving for. Think of distractions as taking the wrong exit on the highway. You have the opportunity to get back on course, but first you have to recognize that you've gotten off track.

On a day-to-day level, distractions are those subtle attention grabbers that pull your attention away from whatever it is that you want to focus on in the moment. Examples of small daily distractions include scrolling through social media, checking your phone every time a notification pops up, texting, or falling down the internet "rabbit hole" of jumping from article to article. Before you know it, the day is almost over and you're wondering, "Where did all the time go?" We've all had days like this, myself included. There are little distractions everywhere just waiting to grab your attention, and you don't have to look very hard to find them. Their ubiquitous nature is what makes them so challenging to fight against. Simple strategies like turning off notifications; turning off the TV, music, or podcast; and eliminating any other distractions can be incredibly helpful when you are trying to focus on what you've prioritized for your day.

An easy way to identify common distractions is to set aside five to ten minutes every night to review your day from start to finish. I encourage you to try this exercise for the next week. Write down everything you did — and I mean everything. Don't let self-criticism or embarrassment prevent you from writing down that you spent forty-five minutes playing your favorite word search game on your phone instead of paying your bills. Think of this list as data-gathering rather than an opportunity to judge or criticize yourself. Once you have your list, go through and identify any distractions that pulled you away from your priority. Once you've identified those distractions, find ways to minimize their effectiveness. For example, let's say you are working on your computer, and you get distracted by an email from a friend or a newsletter from your favorite blogger. Suddenly, your focus shifts from the task at hand. With your concentration broken, it's harder to remember what you were originally focusing on and easier to shift your attention to the distraction. One simple way to help prevent this from happening when you're online (and I speak from personal experience): Consider keeping only one tab open with what you are working on.

Distractions can pull our focus away from our values and priorities in larger and more significant ways, too. The wrong job or an unhealthy relationship are both examples of big distractions. Throwing yourself into work, school, or a relationship at the expense of other areas of your life can also be a distraction. Pouring your energy into something that isn't in line with your values — such as getting a degree that you aren't passionate about because it promises a high-salary job — is also a distraction. So is avoiding identifying your values and priorities in the first place. When we let distractions take over, we get thrown off-balance and off-course from what matters.

Some distractions can be very sneaky and subtle. Early in my career as a therapist, I was eager to gain experience and build up my caseload, so I would take pretty much any client from any age demographic, from small children to clients in their seventies. However, as I progressed in my career, I began to notice a pattern: Those days when I scheduled play therapy or couples' therapy felt more draining. Being a therapist is certainly hard work, but it is also incredibly rewarding and meaningful. However, I began to realize that by focusing on serving everyone, I was missing out on the opportunity to focus on providing the type of therapy I do best: individual therapy to adults. Once I realized where I was being called to focus my skills as a therapist, my work felt even more meaningful than it had before. Making this subtle shift in the way I worked helped me to honor my values and to prioritize so that I could serve my clients to the best of my abilities.

What distractions might be pulling you away from your priorities? To identify them, it can be helpful to make a list of activities in your life that leave you feeling drained. What are those things that cause you to feel dread or discouragement when you see them on your calendar? Write these things down and then try to identify any themes among them. This can point you to the subtle distractions that show up in your life and pull you away from your true purpose.

Another sneaky distraction is the quest for perfection. On the surface, seeking to be perfect looks like a good thing. After all, why wouldn't you want to be the best lawyer, doctor, spouse, friend, mother, employee? While there's nothing wrong with seeking to get better, it becomes a distraction when your focus narrows so that you only see two categories: perfection and failure. Perfectionism is a very black-and-white way of thinking, and it sets up a false dichotomy between success and failure. When that happens, you are no longer focused on becoming the person God is calling you to be. Instead, your focus is on never making mistakes, following rigid rules, and checking off boxes. This keeps you from actively participating in your life.

Brene Brown writes in her book *The Gifts of Imperfection*, "Perfectionism is not the same as striving to be your best. Perfectionism is not about healthy achievement and growth. Perfectionism is the belief that if we live perfect, look perfect, and act perfect, we can minimize or avoid the pain of blame, judgment, and shame. It's a shield." If we want to live a life of authenticity, we've got to let go of the shield of perfectionism. Living the life God invites us to lead includes learning from our mistakes and growing from our failures. Perfectionism doesn't allow for these things.

A final distraction minefield is comparison. Comparing your life to others' lives is a great way to lose sight of your priorities. I love Theodore Roosevelt's often-quoted maxim, "Comparison is the thief of joy," because it perfectly captures the comparison trap. We might be perfectly content with where we are in our lives, but once we start comparing and measuring our lives against what others are doing, we easily become dissatisfied and discouraged, and we lose any contentment or certainty we felt about our path in life. The comparison trap tricks us into thinking that our lives and choices are somehow less than others', and that we have to use the choices that others make as a yardstick to measure our own decisions. We forget that our values and priorities (and, by extension, God's plan for us) should be the yardstick by which we evaluate our lives, and that our life path is completely different from anyone else's in the world. When we compare ourselves to others, we lose the sense of peace, fulfillment, and direction that living an authentic life brings.

Practical Ways to Stay on Track

So far, we've talked about why priorities are an important ingredient in living an active and authentic life, where priorities come from, how to identify them, and what can get in the way of being guided by them. Now, it's time to get really practical and explore ways you can use your priorities as guides on a daily basis and in the larger context of your life.

Remember your "why."

Your priorities aren't arbitrary. Instead, they are a reflection of your values and what you find meaningful in your life. Remembering your "why" will help you stay focused on the path toward the active and authentic life God wants for you. Plus, when things feel tough, remembering the bigger picture and the reason why you even have these priorities can provide much-needed motivation. My insightful editor encouraged me to write down the reason why I am writing this book and to review that statement each time I sat down to write. Not only does it help me stay motivated as I try to figure out the best way to communicate an idea, but it also helps me stay focused on the main ideas of this book instead of taking you down unhelpful tangents.

Write down your priorities.

Perhaps you already have a sense of what your priorities and values are as you read this chapter. That's great! Now go write them down somewhere you can refer to them when needed. Making a list of your priorities (and values) makes them more real and gives you a greater sense of accountability. It's much more difficult to minimize or brush aside a priority when you've written it down. Keep the list somewhere that's easily accessible, whether that's in your journal, in your planner, on the fridge, taped to your mirror, or on your nightstand. Seeing that list often also makes it more difficult to forget those priorities.

Review your priorities.

Once you have your list and you've put it into an easily accessible place, make sure you review your priorities. It might be helpful to take a two-pronged approach: Review them daily to make sure you are ordering your to-do list in a way that honors your priorities. Then spend a little more time monthly and review them to see how they're guiding your life. When you review, ask yourself if each priority is still meaningful to you (in other words, does it still apply to your life circumstances). Are you honoring or incorporating it into your day in the best way possible? These checkpoints allow you to adjust and course correct if needed.

Reflection Questions

- Do I have clearly defined priorities? If yes, what are they? If not, how has the lack of priorities impacted my life?
- After reading this chapter, what are the three to five top priorities I have identified for myself?
- What are the main distractions that prevent me from honoring my priorities and living an active and authentic life?

Action Items

- Write down your top three to five priorities (see Reflection Question 2).
- Set the time you will review your priorities each day. You might consider setting an alarm on your phone to

remind you. Set a monthly calendar date with yourself to review your priorities and make any changes that may be necessary.

4

Decisions, Decisions, Decisions

"What career field should I go into?"
"Do I want to accept this job offer?"
"Should I ask for a pay raise?"
"Should I stay in my current relationship?"
"Should I buy or rent?"
"Should I move someplace new or stay put?"
"Would therapy be helpful for me?"
"Should I continue my friendship with this person?"

Throughout life, we are faced with many decisions, whether it's choosing what to eat for lunch, selecting a career path, or deciding what to do about a relationship. Some decisions seem straightforward and simple, while others can seem incredibly complex.

Making decisions can be challenging. It becomes even more complicated when you factor in our belief as Catholics that God has a specific plan for our life — what we call our "vocation." Making life decisions — especially discerning our vocation — is easier said than done. But the reality is that we simply can't get through life without making decisions. Even if you decide not to decide, you've made a decision!

Cultivating decision-making and discernment skills is key for living an authentic life. Living a meaningful life means that you are actively participating in each moment. You aren't stepping back and letting life just happen to you, but you also aren't holding onto life with a white-knuckled grip. Instead, living authentically means you are always engaged in the present moment, knowing that you can choose how to respond to any situation you might find yourself in and gauge what the best response might be. While it's true that we can't always choose what happens to us, we always have the power to choose how we respond to what happens to us.

Making authentic decisions is a skill anyone can learn and refine over time. While specific decisions can seem pretty complicated, the process of discerning what response is best for you is actually pretty straightforward. I've broken this process down into three steps: observe, reflect, and decide. First, you observe by gathering information about the situation, getting the lay of the land. Second, you reflect on the situation, your values and goals, your options, and any other factors that may contribute to what decision you make. And finally, you decide what response is most in line with your true purpose, based on the factors you identified in the first two steps.

In this chapter, we'll dive into each of these three stages so that you will be equipped to make decisions big and small.

Step 1: Observe
Step 1 in the decision-making process is to gather your data. In

other words, you need to know what you are working with before you can make the best decision.

It can be helpful to ask yourself a few questions:

- What decision am I facing?
- What is the situation or environment surrounding this decision?
- What factors are at play?
- Can the decision be broken into smaller decisions (so that it doesn't feel so overwhelming)?
- What obstacles, if any, are preventing me from making the best decision right now?
- What emotions accompany this decision?
- Is there a time limit associated with this decision?
- What people will be impacted by this decision?
- What are the potential consequences of this decision?

Asking yourself these questions is a little bit like packing for a trip. If you are like me, you gather what you want to pack and lay it all out before you organize it and put it in your suitcase. In this step of observation, you are gathering the pieces of this decision and putting them in one place. You can worry about organizing and editing the pile later. For now, just focus on gathering what you need.

Step 2: Reflect

Once you've gathered all the necessary information in Step 1, it's time to take a closer look at all the factors and consider how they play a role in the big picture of your life. This second step is the analysis stage. A lot can go into even a small decision. That's why it's important to really dive deep and reflect on all the information you gathered. Doing this now can save you time and energy because, when it comes time to make your decision, you will feel confident that you are making the best choice. If you skip this step, you risk making a decision for the wrong reason, whether that be fear, misinformation, or something else. Trust me, it's worth taking the time to really invest in this step.

Feel your feelings.

Your feelings play a critical role in helping you make the best decisions for yourself. Unfortunately, many of us have a complicated or even negative relationship with our feelings. Many of us have been taught to ignore our emotions completely or to view them as "bad." As a result, too many adults have little to no awareness of the many feelings that exist beyond the basic "happy," "sad," and "mad."

Additionally, Catholics often believe that emotions should be removed from any decision-making process because they can lead us into sin and cloud our judgment. Yet our Catholic tradition values emotions and recognizes that they play an important and necessary role in our life. A quick consultation with the *Catechism of the Catholic Church* (paragraphs 1762–1775) reveals that emotions "focus our attention and motivate our actions." In other words, our emotions can direct our attention toward or lead us away from the things that matter. The *Catechism* also says, and this is very important to note, that emotions are neither good nor evil in and of themselves. They only become good or evil once they move us toward a good or evil action. It's up to us to discern whether an emotion is helpful (pointing us toward something good for us) or unhelpful (pulling us away from what is good).

The *Catechism* also tells us that emotions can help us "intuit good and suspect evil" (1771). This is critical for healthy decision-making. For example, let's say a friend asks you to help with her nonprofit fundraiser and you notice that you are feeling overwhelmed by her request. That feeling of overwhelm is a signal that, as much as you'd like to help, you don't have the time or emotional energy right now. The emotion that you were able to identify is pointing you toward what is best for you.

Instead of shying away from our emotions, trying to minimize them, or feeling bad for experiencing them, we can embrace them as important allies in our decision-making process. You might be thinking, "But my emotions always seem to get the best of me. When I am angry, I usually make decisions I regret. When I'm scared, I can never think clearly. How can emotions be neutral, let alone helpful?" The secret to keeping your emotions from running the show is to give yourself time to observe, reflect, and plan before responding. Take the time to notice your emotions, label them, and understand the story they are telling you. This can provide you with invaluable information and help you decide on the best course of action. It's also helpful to approach your emotions with a nonjudgmental attitude of curiosity.

Let's use an example to help illustrate the power of taking the time to reflect on our feelings so that we can make the best decisions.

Jack's job has become increasingly stressful. He was originally hired to develop marketing plans for his firm's clients, but his role has expanded to include working on several in-house projects, and the company culture has taken a dramatic shift. While it used to be a very collaborative, uplifting, and supportive environment, a recent change in upper management has led to a culture of backstabbing, every man for himself, and withholding information. Every morning, Jack dreads going to work and daydreams about quitting on the spot. But he's afraid he won't find another job, so he wants to hold onto this job for as long as he can. Unfortunately, the pressure of the job is starting to take a psychological and physical toll on him. He doesn't know what to do.

To begin, Jack needs to identify the emotions he's dealing with. These include fear, resentment, confusion, sadness, and disappointment. These emotions are telling him how the changes in his workplace are affecting him.

- Jack is feeling fear because he doubts he will be able to

find another job. He might also be experiencing fear related to the unsupportive office climate. What will happen if he makes a mistake? What would the reaction be if he tried to talk to one of his supervisors about his negative experience?

- He is feeling resentment because he is being asked to do more work than he was originally hired to do, and he thinks management views him as a cog in the wheel rather than a human being.
- He is feeling confused because he isn't sure how to respond to these changes at work.
- And he is feeling sadness and disappointment that the job and coworkers he once enjoyed are gone.

Once Jack has gathered this information, he can use it to help him plan what to do next. What his emotions are telling him about his experience can help him generate possible courses of action. Perhaps he should overcome his fear and speak to his boss about how he is feeling; on the other hand, if his fears about the unsupportive environment are justified, he could reach out to a mentor to obtain some guidance on how to proceed. He might start to make a list of the qualities he'd like to find in his next job, and he might even start looking for and applying to open jobs.

Like Jack, you can use your emotions to help gain insight into the decision you are facing, the factors at play, and how you are being affected by the situation you are in. This deeper understanding can help guide you toward making a decision that is in line with your identity, worth, values, and priorities.

Step 3: Decide
In this step, you are using all of the information and analysis from the previous stages to help you identify which decision option is most in line with your true identity and values in life. It may still

be a tough decision to make, but it will mean you are making the decision that is best and most in line with who you are called to be. Let's take a closer look at some of the things you will want to consider in this step.

Be aware of different approaches.

Decision-making is a skill we build with practice throughout our lives, not just in the big moments. In order to be an active participant in the plan God has for you, you need to know how to discern the best course of action to take in any given situation. It's a skill that's essential for living the life God is calling you to lead. If you can't confidently make decisions, you'll likely wind up in one of two extremes: Either you mentally check out and take a very passive approach to life, or you try to control every aspect of your life and avoid anything uncertain. Neither of these approaches leaves room for the intricate dance between the decisions we make and God's plan and invitation to us. The ideal approach is a balanced one that is neither passive nor controlling.

To illustrate, let's look at three fictional college classmates as they search for jobs:

- **The Passive Approach:** Linda, newly graduated with a major in communications, has started the job search process and is already overwhelmed at the sheer number of job posting sites and available jobs. She's submitted her resume to a few companies but hasn't heard back yet. Feeling overwhelmed and discouraged by the whole process, she avoids logging onto any job posting sites and instead contacts her old manager at the local country club where she worked while in college. Although she isn't using her major and feels left out when she hears about her friends' job-hunting successes, she decides to keep the waitressing job and give up on the job search process. When asked why she isn't pursuing a job more in line with her career goals, Linda just shrugs and says that when the right job comes along, she'll take it. Whenever she starts to worry that she hasn't even looked at job postings in weeks, she quickly distracts herself.

- **The Controlling Approach:** Marie, also a communications major, started her job search process the summer before her senior year of college. After hearing horror stories from her older siblings about how tough the job market is, she vowed that she wouldn't be one of those people who "settled" for just any job, so she came up with a plan. She started interning at a marketing agency the summer before her senior year and went back for her month-long Christmas break in order to continue building her resume. Throughout her senior year, she scheduled several informational interviews with alumni in her chosen field. After she accepted a job offer midway through her senior year, she started planning a new spreadsheet with detailed steps to progress in her career. She finds it hard to fall asleep and stay asleep at night because she keeps running over her plan in her mind.

- **The Balanced Approach:** Jenny, another communications major, is also feeling intimidated about the job hunting process. She's heard that the job market is tough right now and that it might be difficult to find a job in her field right out of college. Despite feeling intimidated, Jenny decides on a three-part approach to the process: She will (1) spend an hour each weekday searching for jobs; (2) touch base with her mentor ev-

ery other week; and (3) bring her job search struggles
and questions to prayer each day. Whenever she feels
overwhelmed or discouraged, she tries to put it all in
perspective and remind herself that she is doing ex-
actly what she needs to do to find the best job for her.
It takes her about six months, post-graduation to find
a communications job.

As you can see from these examples, the choices you make about
how to approach a situation strongly influence your experience.
Knowing what approach you tend to take can help you assess
whether — and how — you'd like to change the way you make decisions. For example, if you tend to be a passive decision maker,
perhaps you'd like to focus on being a little more active in your
decision-making approach. If you tend to be more controlling, it
might be helpful to incorporate a little more discernment and de-
tachment in your decisions.

Deciding how you are going to respond to something in your
life is very empowering, especially if you are facing hardship or
inconvenience. One of my favorite champions of this concept
is Austrian psychiatrist Viktor Frankl. In his book *Man's Search
for Meaning*, Frankl describes the time he spent as a prisoner in a
concentration camp during World War II. He noticed that some
of the prisoners seemed to have an inner resolve, and they refused
to become discouraged or hopeless, even in the face of all the horrors and suffering they encountered. Other prisoners lacked this
spirit and instead were hopeless. Frankl wrote that you could tell
who had lost their fighting spirit when they smoked their last cig-
arette. (Cigarettes were extremely rare and valuable in the camps,
so anyone who had one wanted to hang onto it for as long as possible.) Frankl faced unspeakable horrors and sorrow, but he chose
to keep a fighting spirit and look for some kind of purpose, even
in the most horrendous surroundings. We can learn from Frankl

because he lived reality. He wasn't sitting in an ivory tower telling other people noble ways to live their life.

Frankl's wisdom can be applied to anything you are facing in life, the good and the bad. For example, searching for a new job can be an arduous and frustrating process. You can't control when the right job will come along, but you can choose how you are going to approach the job search process. Even if you feel frustrated or "behind" in life, you can choose whether to allow that to be a source of discouragement or a source of motivation. You have the power to choose.

Learn to respond, not just react.
We often respond to situations based on an initial, emotional reaction. When we experience fear or other negative emotions, it's harder to respond based on what is truly best for us. Instead, we react to get away from the negative feeling, rather than making the best decision.

Picture this: You get an email from your boss asking if you can stay late to add edits to a slide deck. You have already made plans with some friends right after work, and saying "yes" means you'll have to cancel. Perhaps your initial reaction is fear of displeasing your boss. But if you quickly respond "Yes, of course," it might lead you to feelings of resentment down the road. Alternatively, you might be tempted to ignore your boss's request in favor of going out with your friends, which could lead to complications with your job or problems in your relationship with your boss.

Either of these may seem like the "best" decision in the moment, but what is the best decision for you in the long term? Instead of going with your initial reaction, consider giving yourself some time to observe, reflect, and plan before making your decision. When you take the time to observe before responding, instead of reacting out of fear or some other negative emotion, you are actively participating in God's plan for your life. Reflecting before deciding creates the opportunity for you to see all potential courses of action and decide which one is most in line with the person God has called you to be. Reflecting may also help you find other options you haven't considered. In the example given above, a third option might be letting your boss know that you already made plans, but that you want to find a way to get your edits done. With a little flexibility and creativity, you might be able to honor your responsibility to your job and your boss, as well as your commitment to your friends.

Focus on the best decision, not the "right" one.
When it comes to discerning and making decisions, bear in mind that the *best* decision for you may not always seem like the *right* decision. The best decision is going to be the one that is in line with your values and the person you believe you are called to be. This may not always line up with other people's expectations for you … or even your expectations for yourself.

Of course, sometimes decisions are black-and-white, such as when we're choosing right versus wrong, especially in matters of faith and morals. But many of the day-to-day decisions we face are not so clear. When we focus too much on making the "right" decision, or the one we think people expect us to make, it is much more difficult to live the authentic life God is calling us to live.

For example, let's say you have an overbearing coworker who routinely pushes work onto your plate that should really be their responsibility. How do you respond to this dilemma? If you have an expectation for yourself that you need to make others happy, it might feel like the right decision would be to take on the work without grumbling, even when you have to stay late to finish up the projects. But is this the best decision? If you dive deeper into your expectation that you have to please people, you might realize that acting this way isn't helping you to be your authentic self. Instead, this expectation lets others dictate your actions instead of you choosing what's best for you. In this case, the best decision is the harder decision, because it means advocating for yourself and the respect you deserve from your coworker.

It takes time and effort to discern the best decision, but it is worth it because it helps you identify how you can act in ways that are in line with the life God is inviting you to lead.

Decision-Making Pitfalls

As we all know too well, it's easy to get stuck when trying to make decisions. As you seek to build a lasting habit of decision-making, it's important to know some of the most common pitfalls so that you can recognize and avoid them. Let's take a look at each of these pitfalls and how they can get in the way of making the best decision for yourself.

Irrational fears

One of the most complicated and powerful emotions that can affect decision-making is fear.

Fear is one of our most basic emotions, alerting us to something that might have a negative impact on us or someone we care about. What makes fear tricky is that sometimes what we fear is legitimately harmful, and sometimes it's not. When our fear is legitimate, it can direct us away from danger and toward safe and healthy decisions. When our fear is not legitimate, however, it can lead us to act in ways that are not really good for us.

For example, say you are in a relationship with someone who has betrayed your trust. You might fear that they will betray your trust again. At the risk of oversimplifying for the sake of this example, let's say your fear is legitimate, especially if that person has not taken steps to amend their actions and restore your trust. Your fear is showing you that you have a legitimate concern and that you should make a decision about that relationship that will restore your sense of safety.

As a counterexample, say you are constantly afraid that your partner will break your trust. But you have no factual evidence of this person ever having done so. In this case, your fear may be pointing you toward anxieties or insecurities that have more to do with your own experiences and inner world than with your partner. Your fear is showing you that you have wounds and insecurities that need to be addressed so that you can enjoy a healthy, trusting relationship with your partner.

When fear is founded in the rational world and facts, it signals that we need to move away from something harmful. But when our fear isn't founded on factual evidence, we need to ask ourselves where it originated and how can we challenge it. That's why it is important to take the time to unpack your fear and identify the meaning behind it. Otherwise, you risk making knee-jerk decisions focused on getting away from whatever is triggering fear, rather than decisions that are best for you in the long term.

Physical and mental stressors

Pay attention to when your physical or mental health is already negatively affected. When you aren't feeling well, it's hard to focus and make the best decision. Even something as simple as being hungry or having a headache can make it very challenging to think about anything other than eating or lying down. In fact, when you aren't feeling your best, being faced with a decision can seem like an annoying inconvenience that you want to avoid or get over as quickly as possible. When you are faced with a decision, even if it seems urgent, it's important to assess your mental and physical state so that you can address anything that might prevent you from making the best decision. The acronym HALT is a helpful guideline for making that assessment: hungry, angry, lonely, tired.

If you are hungry, angry, lonely, or tired, chances are you are not in a good frame of mind to make the decision that's best for you. First, go take care of that feeling; then you can come back to your decision-making. If you are hungry, go grab a snack! If you are angry, take some time to cool down. If you are lonely, reach out to someone in your support network. If you are tired, take a nap or go for a relaxing walk. Once you've addressed these needs, you can continue the decision-making process.

Too many choices

Another potential pitfall when it comes to making the decisions that are best for you is having too many options. It seems like it should be freeing, but having too many choices can actually feel paralyzing. If you've ever taken a psychology course, you may have learned about the "Jam Experiment." In this experiment, researchers set up two different tables of jam samples at a grocery store. One table had six different types of jam to sample, while the other had twenty-four. Research participants were asked to sample the flavors and then choose their favorite. The researchers found that it was easier for the participants to choose their favorite flavor when they were choosing between six flavors rather than when choosing between twenty-four. The same concept applies to other decisions we face in life. When we are presented with an overwhelming number of choices, it can be hard to figure out which is the best choice for us. This can happen when you are considering making a career switch, logging onto a dating app, or thinking about buying a new car. We can get so caught up in exploring every option that we overwhelm ourselves and lose sight of what is best for us.

The key to avoiding this pitfall is to focus on the information you have, rather than letting your attention become consumed by gathering even more information. Then use this information to help you identify what's best for you. For example, if you are thinking about making a career change, instead of taking an endless amount of career assessments, reading a stack of career books, and watching every career coaching video you can find online, pick one or two career books (perhaps based on the recommendation of a respected coworker or mentor) and follow their suggestions. This can help prevent you from feeling overwhelmed and paralyzed when making a choice.

Tying It All Together

As you can see, making a decision is often much more complicated than simply going with your gut or winging it. Instead, making a prudent decision involves a great deal of honest reflection and time before you can determine the best course of action. To help synthesize the concepts covered in this chapter into a cohesive decision-making format, here are some simple questions to ask yourself as you observe, reflect, and plan:

1. What emotions am I experiencing? Are these emotions moving me toward or away from my values? (It should go without saying that decisions that move you away from your values are generally ones you want to avoid.)

2. Am I focused on making the best decision for me, or am I getting trapped in other people's expectations for me or in what I think I should do?

3. Whom can I consult about this decision? Whose perspective and insight do I value? (This is different from asking someone to tell you what to do or having someone make the decision for you.)

4. Is there anything clouding my perspective right now (HALT)? If so, how can I address it before making my decision?

5. Have I prayed for the virtue of prudence yet? Prudence is the virtue that enables us to make practical decisions well. When faced with any decision, it's helpful to ask for the grace of this virtue in prayer.

6. What is the next step I need to take to move me closer to gaining clarity and making a decision? (This ques-

tion is helpful if you are feeling overwhelmed by the prospect of making a decision. Breaking the process down into steps makes the whole thing much more manageable.)

Of course, some decisions are easier to make because we are excited about the outcome. Other decisions are more difficult, because they require us to make tough choices that bring the end of something, such as a job or a relationship, or require hard work on our end, like setting boundaries or addressing unhealthy behaviors in ourselves. But the more you practice the skills we talked about in this chapter, the better equipped you will be to make decisions that align with your values and help you actively and authentically participate in the life God is inviting you to live.

Reflection Questions
- What is my relationship with emotions? Do I view them as allies or enemies? Why?
- Do I tend to take a more passive, active, or controlling approach to making decisions?
- How has fear impacted my decisions in the past?
- What's a difficult decision I am proud of making?

Action Items
- Write down any decisions you have been avoiding lately. Pick one decision and name one step you can take. Make a plan for how and when you are going to take that next step. Don't forget to start small!

5

Establishing Healthy Boundaries

So far, we've explored how crucial it is to know your identity and true purpose; and we've explored expectations, priorities, values, and decision-making. Boundary setting is another valuable tool to help you channel your time and energy toward your purpose. Having clearly defined boundaries, and communicating them in a respectful way to others, helps you to weed out those things that are distracting you from living authentically. In this chapter, we'll take a closer look at what boundaries are, the different types, why they are a valuable tool, and how to implement them.

We use water filters to trap the impurities from our tap water so that our water is sparkling clean and ready to drink. We need a similar kind of filtration system for our lives to help us filter out the distractions and unnecessary drains on our energy that prevent us from actively participating in the authentic life God is calling us to live. We need safeguards in place to keep out anything that distracts us from living our unique calling and fulfilling our mission. Setting healthy boundaries does just that, so we can focus on what really matters in life.

When we don't have clear boundaries in life, it's easy to feel like our circumstances or other people are calling the shots. This prevents us from the active participation and discernment of God's plan that we're trying to cultivate. On the other hand, if our boundaries are too strict, we can't freely participate in God's plan for us because we are too busy trying to control our lives. The answer lies somewhere in the middle: clearly defined, healthy boundaries that empower us to freely and actively participate in our life.

In this chapter, we'll take a look at what boundaries do — and do not — look like, and how they can help you feel less overwhelmed and frazzled by life and more empowered and joyful. We'll also take a deeper look at what can happen when we don't have boundaries or the right kind of boundaries in our lives. We'll also challenge some common misconceptions about boundaries. And finally, we'll use case examples to explore what boundary setting looks like in real life. By the end of this chapter, you will have the tools you need to get started in evaluating your own boundaries.

What Are Boundaries?

The term gets tossed around a lot in therapy circles, and I heard it frequently in my graduate training, but it really wasn't until I read the book *Boundaries* by Drs. Henry Cloud and John Townsend that I had a fuller and more nuanced understanding of what boundaries are. Most of us have heard the term used, but what does it really mean?

Boundaries are the way that you show you have a clear understanding of what is your responsibility and what isn't. They communicate honesty and respect toward yourself and others and facilitate authentic relationships with others.

Boundaries are like guardrails that prevent you from taking on what doesn't need to be your responsibility or from giving away what should be your responsibility. You are responsible for your own emotions, decisions, actions, time, physical space, and energy. You are not responsible for the emotions, decisions, actions, time, physical space, or energy of others (though you are called to respect them).

For example, if you have an argument with a friend and feel angry at him, you are responsible for acknowledging your emotion, for taking responsibility for your role in the argument and what it was about, and for how you choose to respond to it. You are also called to respect your friend, even while you are disagreeing with him; however, you do not have to take responsibility for his words, actions, or emotions. Boundaries help you protect and respect what is yours, and they free you from the unnecessary burden of what is not.

Boundaries apply to all relationships in our lives, including our relationship with ourselves and with God. How boundaries apply will certainly look different depending on your relationship with a particular person, but the principle of boundaries is the same across the board. We'll take a look at how boundaries can be applied in different situations and in different types of relationships throughout the rest of this chapter.

Why Defining Your Boundaries Is Important

When you don't take the time to define what your boundaries are, you risk one of two things happening: Either you feel pulled in every direction except the one you want to go, or you feel isolated and lonely because every aspect of your life is so tightly controlled that there is no room for God's surprises. In the first instance, because you don't have a clear understanding of what is yours and what isn't yours, it's much more challenging to figure out what you want to say yes to and what you want to say no to. Without that clear direction, your boundaries are likely to be more haphazard and sporadically enforced or enforced too late to be effective. On a smaller scale, your day-to-day decisions become dictated by other people or how you are feeling in the moment. On a larger scale, your life doesn't feel like your own because it is influenced by the desires of others instead of your own.

In the second outcome, your boundaries are so strict and rigid that you don't have room for anything other than your own plan for your life. As a result, you are likely to miss out on important relationships and experiences because of your laser focus. Both of these scenarios leave you feeling drained, exhausted, direction-less, and resentful. In the first case, it is because you have given all of your time, attention, and energy to others at the expense of your own needs. In the second case, it is because you have spent all of your time, attention, and energy maintaining strict and rigid boundaries at the expense of authentic connections with others. If this is sounding a little bit like the "Goldilocks and the Three Bears" story, you're not too far off. Having too lax boundaries can be just as harmful as having too rigid boundaries. You want to aim for having boundaries that are in that sweet spot in the middle: firm but with conscious flexibility for when the Holy Spirit prompts you to stray from the plan.

Are Boundaries Selfish?

Especially as Christians and Catholics, we can sometimes confuse setting boundaries with being selfish, putting an unnecessary wall up, or pushing others away — and, therefore, un-Christian. For example, if your church needs volunteers for their latest service project, you might think it's selfish to say that you don't have the time and energy (even though, in reality, you might not). Or, if a family member is asking you to help bail them out of a tough situation over and over again, with no sign of them taking responsibility for their behavior, you might think it's un-Christian to refuse to help them. I'm here to tell you that it isn't selfish or un-Christian to respectfully decline taking responsibility for what God hasn't asked you to take responsibility for — see the list we covered above.

Being a good Christian doesn't mean having zero boundaries. Instead, being a good Christian actually means having healthy boundaries with yourself and others. Putting the needs of others at the expense of your own well-being isn't respecting you or the other person whose needs you are prioritizing. When you do this, your relationship with that person is no longer truly respectful or authentic. Instead, it's saying the other person's needs are more important than yours. Or, depending on the situation, it's saying that your needs are more important than the other person's. The truly selfless approach is to embrace Jesus' command to us, "You shall love your neighbor as yourself" (Mk 12:31). Jesus didn't say, "Love your neighbor instead of yourself" or "Love your neighbor more than yourself." Instead, he puts us on a level playing field, calling us to love and respect both ourselves and our neighbors at the same time. This means taking care of ourselves and respecting our needs in the same way we do for others.

It can also be useful to consider that if we don't recognize our inherent worth and we don't take care of ourselves, how can we be there for others in the way that God calls us to be? Having healthy boundaries enables us to authentically care for others in our lives. Remember that Jesus was known to go off by himself to pray or go with his disciples to be away from the crowds that were clamoring for healing and instruction. And the Good Samaritan didn't care for the injured man himself. He entrusted the man to the care of those who could best take care of him, and once he ensured that the injured man was in the right hands, he went on his way. Those are both examples of what having healthy boundaries looks like. But we can't set healthy boundaries if we don't know our own worth, the worth of our neighbor, what is our responsibility, and what is our neighbor's responsibility.

What does it look like to love your neighbor as yourself with

boundaries in the real world? Let's say you are a chronic oversched-
uler and often arrive late to meetings or plans with friends because
you are running from commitment to commitment. It might be
tempting to argue that rushing and being late is a small price to
pay for being able to do it all and to say yes to every invitation that
comes your way. However, when we take a step back, we can see
that overscheduling yourself and being late is actually the opposite
of showing respect for yourself and others. You haven't taken responsibility for the fact that you only have so many hours in a day,
and even though you'd love to be able to say yes to every invitation
that comes your way, you realistically don't have the time and energy to do that. When you are rushing and running late, you are
telling others that you haven't chosen to extend to them the respect
they deserve. You aren't able to be fully present to the people you are
with or to whatever tasks you have when you are preoccupied with
trying to do it all. (To clarify, we are talking about patterns of being
chronically late.) Another option, which demonstrates respect and
love for those you are making commitments with, would be to only
say yes to invitations that you have time for in your schedule and
to build in plenty of travel time so that you aren't rushing or late —
which means setting some boundaries for yourself.

Types of Boundaries

When you hear the term "boundaries," what comes to mind? For
many of us, physical boundaries are the most common ones we
think of. For example, some people are huggers who are happy to
give everyone they meet, friend or stranger, a warm embrace. Others are not as comfortable with these physical displays of affection.
These are different types of physical boundaries. Boundaries also
extend to other areas of our lives, including our emotions, relationships, energy, and time. Let's take a closer look at these different
types of boundaries.

Emotional

Poor emotional boundaries can lead us to take responsibility for other peoples' feelings at the expense of our own, or to blame others for causing our negative feelings.

Stephen's boss is a mercurial leader who is extremely demanding and who displays frequent angry outbursts. Stephen counts himself lucky to have landed this job and he is eager to make a positive impression on the rest of his team, and especially on his boss. He spends a great deal of time trying to figure out how to anticipate his boss's demands and moods so that he can stay one step ahead of them. When his boss blames him or the team for mistakes that aren't theirs, Stephen and his coworkers find it easier to take the blame in the name of keeping the peace. Stephen is proud of his ability to "manage" his boss's moods, but if he is being honest with himself, it occupies a great deal of his time and takes away from the actual work he's been assigned. He chalks it up to corporate life, but his friends tell him his workplace is a toxic environment.

As Christians, we are called to care for one another and be compassionate toward others. However, this doesn't mean that we need to take on the responsibility of other people's emotional well-being. This also means that we can't place the burden of our own emotional well-being on others. This can be a hard truth to recognize, particularly if you have someone in your life that you care for including children, family members, someone who is disabled or disadvantaged, and so on. You want them to be happy and feel fulfilled in life, but you can't make someone be happy or make someone not be sad anymore. Instead, we are called to be a source of support and encouragement without letting their emotional state serve as a barometer for our own.

For example, if you are in an argument with someone, setting healthy emotional boundaries might look like excusing yourself for a few minutes so that you can cool down, gather your thoughts, and decide how you want to approach the disagreement. Or, if you have a friend who always wants to vent to you and who is looking for you to give them advice or tell them what to do, setting a healthy emotional boundary might look like telling them, "I value you as a friend very much but I am not in a good place to listen to you in the way I'd like to right now. Can we find another time to talk soon?" Setting healthy emotional boundaries frees us to empower ourselves (and others) to embrace our true purpose.

Relational

Poor boundaries in our relationships may lead us to take all of the responsibility for the quality of the relationship instead of seeing it as a joint effort. Or we might leave all responsibility for cultivating the relationship to the other person. Or perhaps there's an imbalance in our relationships regarding needs being met, or a level of emotional connection that isn't appropriate, whether too much or too little emotion.

> Jesse is known as the "dependable one" among his friends. He will answer the phone at any hour to talk when a friend is in distress or drop everything and hop in the car to help a friend in need. Jesse takes pride in being a "good friend," but it is sometimes exhausting to always be available for his friends. He sometimes thinks about blocking off some time for himself, but then feels guilty. He wishes his friends would reciprocate and ask how he is doing or how they can help him with his struggles, but no one seems to even consider that he might benefit from having someone be there for him.

Of course, some people have an easier time setting boundaries than others. You might be reading this and thinking that these ideas seem self-explanatory. For others, these ideas might be radically new and eye-opening. One group of people who tend to struggle the most with setting boundaries are those whom we often call "people pleasers." For those of us who are people pleasers, setting (and sticking to) our boundaries can be extremely challenging because we have been taught through various experiences (society, family, trauma, relationships) that it is more important to help others feel comfortable and happy than it is to pay attention to our own needs. We tell ourselves that we will be happy when we make others happy. For many people pleasers, this translates into giving people in our lives a free pass on our time, energy, and emotions. Unfortunately, this often leaves us feeling drained and resentful toward others because we feel taken advantage of. This is because when we focus on the happiness of others, we neglect to set healthy boundaries for ourselves, which then leads to unbalanced and unhealthy relationships. Sure, others may see us as "dependable" and "easy going," but we feel like a human doormat with everyone stepping all over our time and energy and not reciprocating.

Learning to set healthy boundaries can help bring balance back into your relationships and help you let go of any unhealthy ones. It will require some hard work on your end because you will likely have to wrestle with your own fear of disappointing or upsetting others when you set a boundary for yourself. However, remind yourself that just because someone gets upset when you set a boundary doesn't mean that you are wrong to set that boundary. Instead, it means that the other person isn't respecting the boundary that you are choosing to set. (See how it all comes back to respect?) Boundaries can be a powerful ally in helping you to bring balance and respect back into your relationships.

Physical
This most often applies to dating/romantic relationships, but phys-

ical boundaries are important in any relationship and must be respected.

> *Luke thought it would be fun to have one of his best friends from college be his roommate when he moved into the city for work. However, his friend frequently takes his food without asking and will often burst into Luke's room unannounced when he's on the phone having a serious conversation, napping, or working. His roommate doesn't seem to understand the concept of personal space, but Luke feels awkward bringing it up to his friend because it seems obvious to Luke that they should respect one another's space and possessions. Instead, he finds himself being passive-aggressive and resentful toward his friend, and their friendship is starting to feel strained.*

Physical boundaries relate to our personal space, possessions, and our bodies themselves. We are responsible for discerning what we are comfortable with and what we aren't, and we are responsible for communicating that to others. In the example above, Luke is letting his fear of being "awkward" with his friend prevent him from communicating what he is OK with and not OK with when it comes to borrowing his possessions. His fear is preventing him from being authentic, which is slowly eroding the positive aspects of their friendship. Though it might be an awkward conversation, having a frank discussion about boundaries and expectations as roommates might actually improve the relationship instead of fracturing it. Setting boundaries is never being mean or demanding. It's a form of communication that respects both parties and their needs. If you are not comfortable lending someone something, that is OK. If you aren't comfortable with someone giving you a hug, it's OK. If the pace of a dating relationship is moving too fast and you want to slow things down, that is OK. But remember, it is your responsibility to communicate what you are comfortable or not comfortable with. After all, if you don't communicate your boundaries, how will the other person be able to respect them?

Energy Boundaries

If all of your physical and emotional energy is being funneled into someone else's needs at the expense of your own, or if all of your physical and emotional energy is focused on doing everything in your life perfectly, you probably have some boundary work to do.

> *Rosario has had her life mapped out since grade school. She knew what college she would attend, what she would double major in (biology and philosophy), and where she would go to medical school. She even mapped out target dates for getting married and having children way before she was even dating someone seriously. Having her life all mapped out makes Rosario feel safe and secure. However, there's one small problem: She never seems to find the time to work toward her goals in the way she wants to. Instead, she finds her time being dominated by the needs of her family, her friends, and her boyfriend. It seems like everyone needs something from her whether, it's homework help, running errands for others, tutoring (for free), babysitting her siblings, and supporting her boyfriend's career goals. While none of these things is technically "wrong," things feel out of balance for Rosario because it feels like everyone else's needs take precedence over her own at the expense of her own well-being and what she believes her purpose in life is.*

I call it "The Request." Someone in your life texts, calls, or emails you to say hello, and then asks you to lend your time or expertise and help them out with a project. Now, requesting help from a friend or wanting to collaborate with a colleague aren't necessarily problems, but that doesn't mean you have to say yes to every request that comes your way.

When you are faced with a situation like this, you might be tempted to say yes for several reasons: You might want to be helpful, need to return a favor, feel obligated, or be genuinely excited about the project. But what's the best thing to do? Remember how we talked about using your emotions to gather information before making a decision? The same applies here. What are your emotions telling you about The Request? If you are feeling obligated rather than excited, that may indicate that this particular project is not your responsibility. On the other hand, if you are feeling excited about the opportunity, that may mean that you have the time and energy to take responsibility for this project in your life. You might also want to consider the quality of the relationship you have with the person making The Request.

For example, someone I didn't know emailed me an article they were writing and asked me to read it and share my feedback with them. The topic of the article was only tangentially related to my area of professional expertise, and the request made it seem like I was being asked to edit the article that was going to be published on a site I was unfamiliar with. Given that this request was coming from a relative stranger and that it was asking me to share my professional expertise for free for an unknown publication, I respectfully declined their offer. But I've had other similar requests that I have said yes to. During the COVID-19 quarantine, a good friend and colleague reached out and asked me if I'd be interested in sharing my professional thoughts on practicing self-care during quarantine. Because she was a good friend, I had the time and energy, and the topic was very important to me, I was honored to accept her request and enjoyed participating in the event.

As you can see, many factors feed into deciding what's your responsibility and what isn't, but it's crucial to take the time to weigh them all. In the end, you'll feel at peace with how you respond to a situation, using your knowledge of boundaries.

Time

This might look like being chronically late, overscheduling, frequently canceling commitments you made, or being "on call" at any hour for work, friends, or family.

> *Macie is perpetually exhausted, mentally and physically. Her schedule is so overbooked that she color-coded her planner in an effort to keep some semblance of organization, but just looking at it stresses her out. She's told herself more times than she can count that she will start turning down invitations and professional opportunities in order to restore more balance to her life, but instead she keeps saying yes. Macie feels like she is stuck on a hamster wheel, giving away all of her time to others.*

Overloading your schedule with more commitments than you realistically have time for is a very common example of the need for a boundary. There's a myth, particularly in the working world, that you should take any opportunity that comes your way in the name of gaining experience and showing that you are a team player.

As an intern, I was eager to take on any project I was offered. Many of them were great learning experiences, but I definitely logged many miles on my car and worked irregular hours in order to gain that experience. It wasn't unusual for me to see a handful of clients for therapy for a few hours, followed by a three- to four-hour break, before I had a set of marriage prep sessions to conduct for engaged couples. I loved having the opportunity to be able to do both types of work, but I had to say no to other opportunities so that I could say yes to these. In a similar way, when I was first starting out as a therapist in my first job out of grad school, I was eager to build my caseload up from zero and so I had very long days with odd breaks here and there. I also worked with all age groups so that I could continue to gain experience. Again, there was nothing wrong with my decision to embrace an irregular schedule or to see a diverse population of clients, because I was choosing to relax my time boundaries and I knew the implications of that decision.

However, as I gained more experience and a clearer picture of what my gifts as a therapist were, I started to change my boundaries around time and the type of clients I would work with. I created a schedule that would provide me with more of the work/life balance that I wanted, and that would enable me to work with the populations where I could make the most difference.

I share these examples from my own life because they show how our boundaries shape our experiences by either empowering us or disempowering us. In other words, if your boundaries around time are too flexible, you may wind up feeling exhausted, overwhelmed, and resentful because you have taken responsibility for more than you should have. And if your boundaries are too rigid, you might miss out on important opportunities for growth. With some careful discernment, boundaries can free you to actively and authentically participate in your life, without being held back or pulled in the wrong direction by those things that are demanding your time, attention, and energy.

While this is by no means an exhaustive list, these are the areas that are the most common in my experience. Are there one or more categories that resonate with you? How do your experiences in each of these areas either help or hurt your ability to live an active and authentic life?

Boundaries Self-Assessment

To help you identify what clear and firm boundaries look like, ask yourself the reflection questions listed below. It might even be helpful for you to grab a notebook and pen and write out your responses to these questions. They are designed to get you started thinking about your approach to boundaries in your own life:

- Do I build in time for reflection and discernment before saying yes or no to a request from someone?
- Does saying no to a request come easily to me, or do I struggle with the fear of disappointing others?
- Do I like the balance I have in my life right now, or do I often find myself feeling overwhelmed and over-committed?
- Am I intentional about where I focus my time and energy, or is it dictated by others?
- Do I often feel taken advantage of by others, or am I aware of when someone is asking me to take on something that shouldn't be my responsibility and respectfully decline?
- Does thinking about setting boundaries with others seem intimidating or even selfish?
- Are there situations in which I repeatedly find myself giving more of my time and energy than I originally intended? What do these situations have in common?
- Are there situations I frequently find myself in that make it difficult to be authentically myself?
- Do I find myself asserting my preferences in situations without taking into account the feedback others have expressed to me (this would look like ignoring the boundaries of others)?

I encourage you to dive deep into these questions without fear, even if you have to confront some uncomfortable truths about yourself and your actions. Setting and maintaining boundaries is tough work for many of us, and you are not alone in struggling to establish firm but intentionally flexible boundaries. The questions above should help you identify any problem areas you might have.

By putting strong, flexible boundaries into place, you protect and nurture the talents and characteristics God has gifted to you. And when you are free to direct your time and energy into cultivating those talents, and into authentic relationships with others, you are free to be your most authentic self, the self that God is calling you to be.

Reflection Questions

- What are some times where you set boundaries that were beneficial for you?
- What are some areas in which you struggle to set boundaries? Why do you think this is the case for you?
- How do you think setting healthy boundaries could help you be more authentically "you"?

Action Items

- If this topic really resonated with you, consider diving deeper into these ideas by reading one or more of the many books out there on this topic. A great place to start is with the Boundaries series by Drs. Henry Cloud and John Townsend that I mentioned earlier in this chapter.
- Pick one boundary you'd like to work on getting better at implementing. Make a simple three-step plan (When? With whom? Why?) to help you begin to start using it.

6

Self-Care Comes First

When was the last time you got a good night's sleep? I'm talking about seven to nine hours of blissful, uninterrupted sleep with no screen time or sleep aids, after which you woke up and didn't immediately calculate how many hours were left until you got to sleep again. If you are like most of us, waking up feeling refreshed and well rested either hasn't happened in ages or happens so rarely that it's like an elusive unicorn.

We all know that sleep is important — at least in theory. It not only gives us physical rest, but it also gives our brain the time it needs to clean itself and store memories. Not getting enough sleep can lead to irritability, difficulty concentrating, trouble storing memories and recalling information, slower reaction times, and just general tiredness. The trouble is, while we all know that sleep is important for our mental and physical health, we often don't take the necessary steps to make sure we get the sleep we need on a regular basis.

This disconnect shows up in all areas of our physical and mental health. For instance, we know it's good for us to eat a balanced diet and exercise regularly, but it can be very challenging to make these things into habits. And in theory, we know that it isn't good for us to live with perpetual stress or to leave mental health issues unaddressed, but we feel stuck in the cycle or embarrassed by our needs. It's important to shine a light on this disconnect between what our heads know is good for us and what we actually do with our lives. When we don't prioritize our health, it starts to take a toll on us, wearing us down and causing us to lose sight of who we are called to be. Our quest to live an authentic life becomes clouded by stress, exhaustion, worry, and comparison. We lose focus on what makes us feel whole as human beings created by God.

When it comes to our health, our head tells us one thing, but unless our heart is on board too, we won't be able to make needed life changes, and we'll continue to feel off-center and reactionary rather than centered and empowered. Pay attention to this disconnect between the head and the heart, because it illuminates where we may have a problem, and it can also show us needed solutions. The first, and most important solution, is to move our own health up higher on our priority list. Until we make something a true priority, it's never going to happen in the way we want it to. And that's what this chapter is all about: finding ways to make taking care of yourself a priority.

One of my clients, we'll call him Clark, experienced this disconnect between his head and his heart. He always talked about how he wanted to exercise more. He had read about the physical and mental health benefits of exercise and explored different types of exercise as he considered what he'd like to try. He would talk about joining a gym, taking kickboxing classes, running, or just buying a few sets of weights to create a home gym. But Clark never actually started to exercise. In our sessions, we'd come up with a concrete plan for starting to train for a 5K that included which days he'd run, what time of day, and what he could do to motivate himself, but those plans never materialized. Clark sincerely wanted to work out and take care of his health, but he struggled to put it into action. After we worked together for a time, Clark finally got to a place where he decided to make exercise a priority and just get started. That day he went home, put on his running shoes, and went for a walk interspersed with some jogging around the neighborhood. From that moment on, Clark was able to maintain a commitment to exercising three or four times a week. Of course, he had days that were easier than others, but once he eliminated that disconnect between his head and heart and made exercise a priority, he never looked back.

God has given each of us a unique set of talents and gifts that he is inviting us to nurture and use, but we cannot effectively embrace this call when we are stressed, tired, and not living a healthy lifestyle. And this is where self-care comes in.

Self-care at its simplest is any practice that promotes your physical, mental, emotional, relational, or spiritual well-being. There is a common misconception that self-care is all about "treating yourself," but authentic self-care is actually a discipline that honors who we are as beings created in the image and likeness of God — mind, body, and soul. We need to take care of our mind, our body, and our soul in order to really flourish and thrive in life and to wholeheartedly answer God's invitation in our lives.

Not only does authentic self-care honor that we are loved unconditionally by God, but it also protects against the effects of stress which, if left unchecked, can sneakily pull us away from living life authentically. When we're stressed, it's much more challenging to live an authentic and active life in alignment with God's plan. In fact, it's sometimes hard to figure out what God's plan even is when we're so stressed. Stress clouds our judgment, confuses our priorities, and makes it difficult to make the best decisions. It keeps us stuck in a negative cycle, spinning and spinning but going nowhere.

Stress is everywhere. In fact, more than 75 percent of adults report experiencing physical or emotional symptoms of stress in the past month, and 42 percent of adults say that they aren't doing enough to manage the negative effects stress has on their lives.[13] Those two statistics paint a powerful picture of how damaging the disconnect between our head and heart can be. We know we're stressed, but we feel too overwhelmed and paralyzed to do anything about it.

Part of the reason why we feel paralyzed and overwhelmed by stress is because it activates a physical response from our body. When our body determines that something is harmful to us — whether that be an argument with a significant other, an impending deadline at work or school, or narrowly avoiding a car accident (just to name a few) — it activates our sympathetic nervous system. Think of this system as akin to pressing down on a car's gas pedal and accelerating rapidly. When this system is activated, our heart rate increases, breathing becomes shallower, muscles tense, and digestion slows. Some people might feel a tightness in their chest, get tunnel vision, or have racing thoughts. All of this is because the body is preparing to fight, flee, or freeze to reduce the chance of being harmed. These physiological changes are meant to protect us from harm, whether real or perceived. When the body senses that the danger has passed, it activates the parasympathetic nervous system, which is like pressing down on the brake pedal of a car. The heart rate slows down, breathing deepens, muscles relax, and thinking becomes calmer and clearer. The sympathetic nervous system can only be activated when our body and brain sense that we are safe again.

If you are constantly being exposed to stress in your life, your body and brain are doing one of two things: Either (1) they are waffling back and forth between ramping up to respond to stress,

---

[13] https://www.apa.org/news/press/releases/2007/10/stress

winding down, and then ramping up again; or (2) they are stuck in a state of constant arousal because of the sheer number of stressors you are exposed to. In both cases, the effects of stress start to wear you down because you don't have the time you need to recharge and restore before the next stressor comes along. The negative effects start to build up and take a toll on your mind and body. Common signs of stress include the following:

- Headaches
- Muscle tension and/or back pain
- Upset stomach
- Rapid heart rate
- Difficulty falling asleep or staying asleep
- Fatigue
- Changes in appetite (loss of appetite or increase in "stress eating")
- Weakened immune system
- Difficulty concentrating
- Memory issues (difficulty forming new memories or recalling old memories)
- Feeling "on edge" or jumpy
- Irritability
- Anxiety or constant worrying

I remember one of the first times I experienced stress impacting me physically. It was my first semester as a freshman in high school, and it was finals week. I had no idea what to expect, since I'd never taken a proper final exam before, and I wanted to do well. If you had asked me if I was nervous about finals week, I probably would have told you yes, but I would have rated my level of concern as maybe a 4 or 5 on a scale of 1 to 10 (with 10 being the most nervous). But I had this mysterious and terrible back pain the whole week. Once I completed my last final exam of the semester, the back pain suddenly disappeared. I realized that it had been stress-related muscle tension, and my stress over my exams had been much greater than I originally thought. My body was trying to be helpful and absorb some of the stress I was experiencing so that I could plow through finals week. This was also a wake-up call to my fourteen-year-old self that I needed to keep an eye out for future symptoms of stress so that I could address it as soon as possible.

When we're in a state of constant stress, it's very difficult to think of anything other than how stressed we are. This is because all our mental, emotional, and physical resources are being poured into surviving, putting any thoughts of thriving on hold. When this is our reality, we can't take an active and authentic role in God's plan for our life, because all our physical and mental resources are being diverted elsewhere. This is why, if we're not careful, stress can take over our life and cloud our ability to lead the life we want. Here's the good news: Self-care is the antidote to stress and the secret to being able to maintain an active approach to life and God's plan. Self-care serves as the protective buffer between us and the effects of stress.

So what does self-care look like if it isn't bubble baths, massages, and manicures? As mentioned above, practicing self-care means choosing strategies and activities that support your physical, mental, emotional, relational, and spiritual well-being. And before you start to feel stressed at the thought of addressing all five of these areas at the same time, it's important and helpful to note that addressing just one of these areas will have a spillover effect and benefit the other four areas. Additionally, self-care isn't about having the perfect plan, nor does one size fit all. Instead, it's best to decide your approach based on your season in life, your personality, and which area of self-care you think you'd benefit from focusing on the most. For example, an introverted person will most likely enjoy introspective self-care activities such as journaling, reading, or going for walks on their own, while an extroverted person might prefer to work out with a friend, join a book club, or try out a new event. Focus on a self-care routine that works best for you and focus on incorporating small strategies rather than overhauling your whole schedule and life in the name of self-care.

What do you do if you know that authentic self-care is good for you but you are having trouble making it a priority in your life? In addition to focusing on personalizing your routine and starting small as I mentioned earlier, it might be helpful to reflect on these questions:

- What is holding you back from implementing a self-care plan? A scheduling issue? The belief that you aren't worthy? Mistaking self-care for being self-indulgent?
- What can you do to help make this hurdle smaller (or disappear altogether)?
- What excuses and "but" statements come to your mind when you think about starting a self-care activity?
- Are there any misconceptions about authentic self-care that are preventing you from implementing a self-care plan?
- Are you creating a plan that fits your lifestyle and goals?

To help get you started with a self-care plan, the following are some suggestions for strategies and activities for each of the five areas of self-care:

Physical Self-Care
- Eliminate screen time before bed.
- Establish a bedtime routine.
- Get seven to nine hours of sleep a night.

- Establish a consistent schedule for sleeping and waking.
- Eat regular meals (avoid skipping meals).
- Prepare home-cooked meals five nights a week.
- Go for a walk with a friend twice a week.
- Sign up for an exercise class with a friend (or go on your own).

Mental Self-Care

- Challenge negative thinking patterns that contribute to stress or worry.
- Monitor social media use.
- Focus on activities and self-talk that increase your confidence.
- Establish time to decompress and recharge each day.
- Take up a new hobby (and make time for leisure).

Emotional Self-Care

- Use relaxation strategies such as deep breathing or stretches.
- Practice being present.
- Practice gratitude.
- Journal.

Relational Self-Care

- Cultivate supportive and authentic relationships.
- Set healthy boundaries.
- Let go of unhealthy relationships.
- Build healthy communication skills.

Spiritual Self-Care

- Meet with a spiritual director.
- Join a women's or men's group.

- Establish a prayer routine.
- Start a spiritual reading practice (or listen to spiritual podcasts).
- Learn more about the lives of the saints.

While this is by no means an exhaustive list, it's meant to help you start to generate your own ideas based on what you think you need the most. To help illustrate what implementing a self-care plan looks like and how it can be beneficial, let's take a look at Melanie's story.

Melanie had an emotionally difficult job in advocacy and a demanding boss who expected her to take on any task, including many that were not on her initial job description. She was frequently asked to return phone calls and run errands after her coworkers went home for the day, and she often had to attend special events on the weekend, which cut into plans with friends and her boyfriend. This was starting to cause tension in her relationships, and Melanie felt caught in the middle. She wanted to be a good employee and team player, but she also missed her friends. Her busy, unpredictable schedule and her slowly diminishing personal life were starting to keep her up at night with worry. She lost her appetite and began to dream about quitting dramatically, packing up, and moving to a completely different state. Melanie was heading toward burnout, and she knew she had to do something. She came to see me, and together we came up with a simple self-care plan to get her started. She established a bedtime routine that included journaling and listening to calming music before bed; she set clear time boundaries with work after hours (beginning with setting up an automatic out-of-office reply on her email); and she prioritized time with her friends and boyfriend as best as she could. These changes made a significant improvement in Melanie's well-being. Once they became habits, she felt empowered to incorporate other self-care strategies like attending daily Mass once a week and exercising. And she no longer dreamt about running away from work and moving to another state.

Melanie's story shows how tangled and trapped stress can make us feel. She couldn't even think about thriving or living authentically because she was so busy just trying to survive. But her story also demonstrates how making just a few small but powerful changes can help us start to untangle ourselves from stress and free us to feel like ourselves again. Self-care strategies are a foundation upon which we can build our life and open ourselves up to becoming the people God created us to be.

Reflection Questions
- In what ways is stress negatively affecting your life right now?
- What self-care strategies are you already using?
- Which of the five areas of self-care do you need to focus on?

Action Items
- Pick one category of self-care that you want to work on.
- Pick one strategy you would like to implement from the category you chose.
- Try that strategy today!

7

Owning Your Worth

We all know someone who has that indescribable air of confidence. They are authentic in everything they do and have a strong sense of purpose that affects the way they speak, the way they carry themselves, and the way that they spend their time. One of those people in my life is a fellow therapist and colleague. She knows who she is, and this is infused into her personal life and her work with her psychotherapy clients. But she is also realistic and vulnerable about her own struggles and doubts, even while she empowers herself and others. Her confidence comes not from being perfect, but from knowing her purpose and living out that purpose in an authentic way. She lets her values guide her decisions, she challenges faulty expectations, and she sets boundaries to help her honor what's important to her.

When we don't have a strong sense of our worth and purpose, it's hard to know where we want to go in life, where to direct our energy, and how to spend our time. This makes it hard to feel confident about our life, because we don't know where to focus. As a result, many people suffer from impostor syndrome, worrying that sooner or later everyone will find out that they are faking it, and that they actually have no idea what they're doing in life. Research on impostor syndrome estimates that 70 percent of people have experienced this feeling at least once in their life. Have you ever felt this way?

The secret to finding your own sense of authentic confidence is knowing and owning your worth. Now, knowing your worth isn't a cheesy greeting card platitude. It also isn't about being perfect. Instead, it's about knowing who you truly are and the source of your worth. We'll dive deeper into where a true and authentic sense of self-worth comes from later in this chapter, but first, we need to look at what your worth *isn't* based on.

Your worth is *not* based on:

Your achievements

This is a tough one! Many of us learned early on that our achievements made us worthy of love and attention. We learned to chase praise and recognition, pushing ourselves to accomplish more and more to win the approval of our loved ones, our teachers, and even our peers. Yet getting that approval always seems to be a moving target that we never reach. There's always something more we could be doing, and this is incredibly discouraging. No matter how many straight A's you get, the number of digits on your paycheck, the number of followers you have on social media, or the prestige associated with your chosen career, there will always be something more you can achieve. You'll never feel satisfied. Of course, it's not wrong to pursue excellence and do your best. But no amount of achievements can ever be the measure of your worth as a person.

Your appearance

We tend to focus on our appearance as a means by which we can feel worthy and accepted both by ourselves and others. Our inner critic whispers that if we can just look a certain way, then we'll be beautiful and desirable, worthy of acceptance and love. As a result, many people today struggle with body image issues. This affects both men and women alike. One study found that 41 percent of men thought they were too heavy and were self-conscious about their weight, and 11 percent reported thinking they were unattractive.[14] One study found that although 73 percent of the women in the study were considered "normal" weight, 71 percent of them expressed a desire to be thinner.[15] Another study found that 23 percent of adult women in the United States reported frequently checking their weight or trying on clothes to see if they fit, and 11 percent reported avoiding looking at their body.[16] More severe cases of body image dissatisfaction can lead to an eating disorder, and research estimates that more than thirty million people in the United States suffer from an eating disorder.[17]

The trouble with placing so much pressure on ourselves to look a certain way is that we are reducing our worth to only our physical appearance, forgetting that we are body and soul. The reality is that your physical appearance is just one aspect of what makes you you, and you should never feel like you have to conform to some arbitrary standard. Instead, your appearance should be an outward reflection of how you feel in your heart about yourself and your worth: that you are created and loved by God.

How you measure up to others

It's normal to look to others to get a sense of the decisions and directions we should take for our lives. This form of crowd-sourcing can even be helpful as we seek to figure out our career or discern major

---

[14] https://psycnet.apa.org/record/2006-22420-012
[15] https://pubmed.ncbi.nlm.nih.gov/9547663/
[16] https://www.ncbi.nlm.nih.gov/pmc/articles/PMC2696560/
[17] https://www.eatingrecoverycenter.com/blog/advocacy/Eating-Disorder-Statistics
-NEDA-Week-2020

decisions in our lives. However, looking to others can get us into trouble when we start comparing ourselves to them. Comparing ourselves to other people is false, because it assumes that one person must be better than the other. Either we end up looking down on others, or we find that we never measure up. We can't measure our characteristics, appearance, hopes, dreams, and talents against those of others, because they and we are completely unique. It is far more helpful to look to those you trust for inspiration and guidance, recognizing that it isn't a competition. Our worth does not come from being "better" than other people (however we might measure that). God created each one of us to be our own person, and there is room for each one of us in his plan.

Your expectations

Our expectations can give us a false sense of worthiness or unworthiness. When we have a rigid idea of what we need to do, say, or look like in order to be found worthy by ourselves, others, and God, either we feel like we are perpetually falling short of that mark, or we relentlessly pursue it at the expense of our overall well-being. For example, we can get stuck in the mindset that there is only one way to be a "good Catholic" or a "good Christian." Whether we receive that message from our family, friends, or faith community, when this happens, we believe that our worth depends on praying certain prayers, engaging in certain types of media or following particular thought leaders, going on mission trips, working for a nonprofit, or going to a certain type of church. Yet when we let these expectations become our guiding star, we lose sight of what it really means to be people of faith. Life starts to feel more like squeezing ourselves into a rigid mold or checking off boxes. If there was really only one way to be a good Christian, how could we have such a diverse collection of saints? There's not just one way to live a holy and authentic life. Take a moment to reflect and ask yourself what expectations might be hemming you in. Do your expectations leave room for you to express and use the talents and characteristics God has given you, or are they too narrow?

Your goals for the future

Have you ever said to yourself, "I'll be happier and feel more worthy when I ..."? When we tell ourselves we'll only feel good about ourselves once we achieve something in the future, we necessarily imply that our current self isn't enough. Just as placing our worth in achievements can backfire, placing our worth in one change that we hope to make puts a great deal of pressure on being successful in realizing that change. It creates a dichotomy where our worth is entirely based on our relative success in implementing that goal. It doesn't leave any room for us to discover our true worth right now.

Being perfect

Many of us try to secure our worth by attempting to be "perfect." We all know, in theory, that it's impossible to really be perfect (hello, original sin), but we also know that we are called to continually strive for excellence. Though it isn't necessarily unhealthy to strive to improve, it *is* unhealthy to associate our worth with a goal we won't truly reach until eternity — and it's especially unhealthy to chase the world's version of perfection. We'll never feel good enough and may even start to believe that our inability to achieve perfection is a sign of our lack of worth. See how messy it can get?

A more authentic approach to self-improvement would be to always strive to do better, but with an understanding that we will make mistakes and fall along the way no matter how hard we try. Remember that you are a work in progress, and you are seeking to become an increasingly authentic version of who God created you to be. Your worth doesn't lie in being perfect and never making mistakes — and similarly, your mistakes don't take away from your inherent value. It's about the intent of striving to consistently be better than before and more in line with your true calling than before. In fact, the *Catechism* says, the human person "finds [their] perfection 'in seeking and loving what is true and good.'" (1704) If we are always seeking what is true and good, then we are pursuing our true purpose.

When one or more of these things define our sense of worth, we reduce our experience as a human being to something far too narrow. We are much more than our appearance, paycheck, or achievements — but it's so easy to forget that.

How do these false measures of worth show up in your life? None of us is immune to them, so be encouraged: You are not alone in your struggle. Ask yourself if one or more of these measures is currently serving as your primary source of worth. If it is, how is it holding you back from being your authentic self?

Now let's take a look at the *true* source of your worth: who you are. Notice that all the measures explored above focus on what you *do*, not on who you *are*. When you focus instead on who you are, you'll find a much stronger and more authentic source of worth.

Who Are You?

How would you answer this question, which I posed in the first chapter? You might say you are a son or daughter, a friend, an employee, a student, a coworker, an athlete, an activist, a missionary, a singer, an artist, a Christian, a Catholic, a nonbeliever, and the list could go on and on. All these qualities are important in their own way, but the most important and most meaningful answer to this question is that you are a daughter or son of God, created in his image. While all these other qualities describe some aspect of who you are, none of them can fully capture what it means to be you. Only being a child of God can do that. This is your strongest and fullest source of worth.

Let's take a look at what the *Catechism* says about who we are:

The divine image is present in every man. ... Endowed

with "a spiritual and immortal" soul, the human person
is "the only creature on earth that God has willed for its
own sake." ... The human person participates in the light
and power of the divine Spirit. By his reason, he is capable of understanding the order of things established by
the Creator. By free will, he is capable of directing himself
toward his true good. He finds his perfection "in seeking
and loving what is true and good." ... Everyone is obliged
to follow this law, which makes itself heard in conscience
and is fulfilled in the love of God and of neighbor. (CCC
1702–1706)

Now, let's unpack what we just read.

First of all, God intentionally created you out of love. No matter how low you are feeling on one of your most challenging days,
never forget that you were created by Love itself. In his book *Life of
Christ*, Venerable Fulton Sheen says, "Why is anyone lovable — if
it be not that God put His love into each of us?" We were created
by God because he loves us, and being loved by God gives us more
worth than any semblance of perfection we could achieve on our
own. Being loved by God is the richest and most authentic source
of worth that we could ever hope to find. And because his love is
unconditional, there is nothing we can do, good or bad, to influence or change it. When we make mistakes, God extends forgiveness and mercy. When we are struggling, God is compassionate
and is present with us in our moments of suffering. We aren't alone,
even at our most imperfect. God's love for us paints a very different
picture of our worth. Our worth as a child of God never changes
and is therefore secure — unlike a sense of worth based on any
other measure.

When you base your worth on God's unchanging love for you,
you never have to prove your worth. Nothing you can do can add to
or subtract from God's love for you. This frees you from any anxi-

ety or pressure you might experience about proving your worth to yourself or anyone else.

We have many examples of God's love for us as individuals. In the Gospel of Luke we read, "Are not five sparrows sold for two pennies? And not one of them is forgotten before God. Why, even the hairs of your head are all numbered. Do not be afraid. You are worth more than many sparrows" (12:6–7). God's love for us never wavers, not even for a second. But often when we are struggling, we feel as if God is very far away from us, or even that he is punishing us for our failures. Instead, we have to remember the message Jesus shares with us in the Gospel. Jesus tells us that when we encounter suffering, it doesn't mean that we are worth any less. Sometimes we fall into the "prosperity gospel" mindset, believing that God showers blessings on those he loves the most, and that our blessings are a sign of God's approval.

The absence of suffering has nothing to do with our holiness or worth. The reality is, we all encounter suffering at some point in our lives (some more than others). Jesus shows us that even in our sufferings, God is still loving us, and thanks to Jesus' death on the cross, our sufferings can even have merit if we unite them with his. Don't forget Jesus' agony in the garden, where he prayed that God the Father spare him from suffering. And remember Mary, standing at the foot of the cross, watching her Son die. Jesus, the Son of God and second Person of the Trinity, experienced suffering and grief; and Mary, born without original sin, also suffered. Think about all the saints whose suffering was a formative part of their story. Saint Ignatius of Loyola experienced his conversion while he was healing from battle wounds. Saint Bernadette was ridiculed for saying she had had a vision of Mary. Saint Martin de Porres was initially denied entry into the Dominican order because of the color of his skin, and experienced discrimination by brothers in the order. God loves us equally, whether we are having a good day, a rough day, or just an OK day. He loves us the same no matter what happens.

What does life look like when we live according to the belief that who we are matters more than what we do? It looks like allowing this knowledge and conviction to infuse our actions and give them deeper meaning. When we approach life this way, we embrace the command to "love your neighbor as yourself" (Mk 12:31), because we operate from the conviction that our worth and our neighbor's worth come from being loved by God. Suddenly, our job title and relationship status don't matter nearly so much. Instead, we focus on how we live on a daily basis in the current season of our life.

The Little Way

One of the saints who offers the greatest example of living out everyday life based on her true worth is Saint Thérèse of Lisieux. She is a popular saint (in fact, she's my confirmation saint!), and her message can come across at first as far too sweet and dainty. Yet she is a Doctor of the Church for good reason. Thérèse was incredibly aware of her sinfulness and her weaknesses, but she never doubted God's immense love for her. Even when she went through an intense period of spiritual dryness and darkness, her belief in God's love for her never wavered. She strove to live out what she called the Little Way, which is to do everything with love, no matter how small or mundane the action might be. Her way of living was simple but profound, transforming the motivation behind every action in her day. Following her Little Way, housework can become an act of love. The boring tasks of your job can become an act of love. When your relationship is in a rough patch, you can continue to strive to make things right out of love (this does not apply to abusive relationships). Thérèse realized that simple tasks, no matter how small or mundane, take on great meaning when we do them out of love.

When Thérèse passed away from tuberculosis at age twenty-four, one of the other sisters in her community commented that they would have nothing of note to write in her obituary because her life had been so unremarkable. Of course, once her autobiography became widely distributed, she was recognized for her remarkable holiness, and for showing all of us how to live out our faith every day.

Following Saint Thérèse's Little Way can help us stop looking for our worth in all the wrong places. Instead, we can start living life in the way God intended right now. As Mother Teresa said, "Do small things with great love." When we live with this intent, we begin to find meaning and purpose in life.

Basing our worth on God's love for us instead of other false measures is unchanging and long-lasting. We can base our worth on God's love for us without fearing that it can be taken away or changed. When we do this, we can live each moment confidently, knowing that we are worthy because God loves us. This gets to the core of what it means to be fully human and to flourish: to live life out of love and not out of fear.

The concepts presented in this chapter are big ideas, and you might be feeling overwhelmed at the prospect of uprooting old ways of thinking about and seeking worthiness. It will take time to start to untangle old patterns of thinking and living and to embrace new ones. Don't be discouraged; simply embrace taking one step at a time. Take your time and ask God to accompany you on this journey of better understanding and believing in his love for you.

As you start taking small steps, making different choices, and reorienting your sense of self-worth, you will start to notice that you are thinking differently, feeling differently, and interacting with others differently. You will start to become more and more like those people you admire for radiating confidence and being convicted in the purpose they have been given. When we start to recognize the source of our true worth, God's love, we start to see ourselves, others, and our relationships in a completely different way. This translates to a shift in how we interact with others, including with whom we spend our time with, how we respond to others, and how we treat ourselves. Before you know it, you just might be one of those people about whom people wonder, "What is her secret to her authenticity and confidence?"

Reflection Questions

- What do you tend to base your worth on?
- What experiences and relationships in your life have led you to base your worth on those things?
- What is the result of basing your worth on those things? Where has it led you?
- How difficult or easy is it for you to believe that God loves you unconditionally? Why do you think that's the case?
- Who is someone in your life who radiates God's love for them? How can you tell?

Action Items

- Make a list of the situations or thoughts you have that make it difficult for you to believe God's love for you. Pick one item on that list and spend some time reflecting on it. Then try to identify either actions or alternative thoughts to help you avoid basing your worth on this particular thing in the future.
- Choose a saint who inspires you to serve as the patron saint of your journey toward more deeply believing in God's love for you.
- What are some experiences or relationships that you've had that have helped you see God's love for you? Make a list of these and keep them handy to review when you struggle to believe in your worthiness.

8

Real-World Challenges to Living Authentically

A few years ago, I had the opportunity to participate on a panel at the SEEK conference about the challenges of friendship in the digital age. As I looked out at the faces of the young adults in attendance, it struck me how much they desired to live an authentic life that's driven by a strong sense of purpose. I had the privilege of meeting several of them after the presentation, and one overwhelming theme emerged in the stories they shared with me: They wanted to live an authentic life, but they felt they could not for a variety of reasons. Some felt that they didn't know how. Others were facing challenges in their life that made it hard for them to be free to live with purpose. Still others didn't feel confident in their abilities to accomplish what they felt they were called to do. All of them were searching for the answers. Yet they didn't give up hope. They chose to keep exploring and to keep believing that they would find

113

freedom to live life purposefully. As so often happens when I give presentations, I left feeling like I had received so much more than I gave. These young adults inspired me with their resilience and their passion.

If you are facing challenges in your life and are searching for a way to live with purpose, you are not alone. Young adults today are facing many different factors that make living an authentic life challenging and confusing at times. These come from external factors — such as cultural and societal influences and family backgrounds — and from within our own hearts and minds. We have to battle these influences if we want to live according to the purpose we've been given by God. For the rest of this chapter, we'll take a look at some of the most common challenges young adults are facing today, both internally and externally. Then we'll use the rest of this book to dive into ways we can push back on these influences so that they don't negatively impact our lives.

External Factors

There's no doubt that the world we live in shapes the direction of our lives. Whether it's an economic recession, cultural trends, or societal beliefs, what's going on in the world around us influences the way we think about and interact with ourselves, others, and the world as a whole. Often we are not even aware of how much these factors impact us, in good and bad ways. You've heard the saying, "Knowledge is power," and that certainly applies to these influences. When you are aware of how these factors affect your life, you have the power to make necessary changes to weaken any negative influence they have. Let's explore some of the more common external factors that can cloud our sense of identity and purpose.

The narrow definition of success

Our culture tends to promote a singular definition of success: pursuing whatever will help you achieve wealth, recognition, and influence. These three ingredients are the recipe for success according to subtle (and not-so-subtle) messages we receive in our formative years and in workplace culture. Achieving success based on society's rules reduces our purpose to chasing money and power. This can affect us in little ways — like placing importance on the number of followers we have on social media — and it can affect us in big ways, influencing not only our career, but also our relationship choices. When we allow this definition of success to drive our choices, we miss out on a richer and more authentic way of life.

The *"life is a competition"* myth

Our society treats life like a competition for a limited amount of resources. This survival-of-the-fittest mindset traps us into seeing others as obstacles to be overcome in our quest to win. If we're not confident about our own purpose and abilities, this competitive way of thinking can lure us into the comparison trap. Inevitably, comparison either leads us to feel like we fall short or to falsely inflate our sense of self-worth by putting others down. Either way, viewing others as competition or as objects of comparison removes the focus from our calling in life and our sense of community, and turns the focus onto what we or others lack. It drives a wedge between us and our community as we compete from a scarcity mindset.

Consumerism

In the Gospels, we encounter the rich young man, who approached Jesus to find out what he needed to do to gain eternal life. We read that he "went away sorrowful" (Mt 19:22) after Jesus told him to "go, sell what you possess and give to the poor, and you will have treasure in heaven" (19: 21). There's a reason why St. Francis of Assisi's decision to renounce his wealth to give his life to serve God was considered radical (and still is). Throughout human history, we have placed a huge emphasis on material possessions. They can provide a sense of comfort and security, true, but they can also take up a larger part in our lives than they should. When this happens, possessions can become the focus of our lives. We get wrapped up in having the latest phone or gadget or the most current style of clothing. These things aren't wrong in themselves when approached with moderation, but when they become our source of identity and purpose, they are deeply problematic. Consumerism can make us forget the First Commandment: "I am the Lord your God, you shall have no other gods besides me."

The "do what feels good" mentality

We've all heard these messages from the culture: "Treat yourself" and "Do what feels good." We're encouraged to take an egocentric and reactionary approach to life. Do what's best for me, even if that's at the expense of others. Do what feels good in the moment, and don't bother to take the time to observe, reflect, and discern before taking action. The trouble with this approach to life is that you prevent yourself from being able to go deeper. When you react from emotion, you can't discern the best course of action, the one that's most in line with your authentic self and true purpose. Instead, you're stuck at a surface level where whims or external pressures push and pull you this way and that. Instead of being guided by fleeting emotions, ask, "What is the best thing to do that is in line with my true purpose?" It might still mean taking time for yourself, doing something fun, or taking a break. But by asking this question, you are giving yourself the opportunity to intentionally choose what's best, instead of just going with the flow.

Moral relativism

Moral relativism is the idea prevalent in our society today that there is no objective truth. According to this view, "truth" can be different for each of us. This worldview is deeply harmful to those who are looking to live a life of purpose and authenticity, because it leaves each of us to construct our own "truths" and purpose, instead of being able to work from within the framework of objective truth. Although it's true that we all have our own opinions and thoughts about people, world events, experiences, solutions, and so on, there is such a thing as objective truth. To deny this is to deny what Christ himself has taught us through his Church. If we want to live a life of purpose and authenticity, then we need to have a clear understanding that truth exists, and that it's our responsibility to think critically and seek the truth in all situations.

Changes in milestones

In the introduction, we talked about how many young adults are getting married, having children, and buying homes later in life than previous generations. While some young people make these choices intentionally, many are influenced by economic factors, including lower earnings and job uncertainty. The expectation of working for one corporation with great benefits is a thing of the past for many young adults. Instead, downsizing and other factors can mean young adults hop from job to job for a long time, making it difficult to "settle down" with a family or make other long-term commitments. These shifting milestones and expectations can be a source of disappointment and frustration.

Internal Factors

While cultural and societal factors certainly influence the way we live, many internal factors — such as our core beliefs, perfectionism, fear of vulnerability, entitlement, mental health, faith struggles, people pleasing, and the reality of sin — can be even more impactful as we seek to live our lives with purpose. These internal factors shape the way we think about ourselves, our ideas about what a life of purpose means, and our confidence (or lack thereof) in our ability to live an authentic life.

Core beliefs

Our own thoughts and beliefs influence us deeply. The core beliefs we have about ourselves and other people serve as the basis or starting point for most of our thoughts and actions. For example, many of us believe, "I am not lovable," and our actions are a response to this belief. Someone with this core belief might feel lonely or struggle to make friends because they have a difficult time believing that other people actually want to be their friend. Other core beliefs can include:

- I am not enough.
- Other people aren't dependable and can't be trusted.
- My past mistakes define me, and I will never overcome them.
- I am too sinful to be a good person.
- Others are better than I can ever hope to be.

Identifying your core beliefs and how they impact you is an important part of setting yourself free to live an authentic and purpose-filled life.

Perfectionism

Do you have a deep-seated fear of making mistakes? Do you struggle to acknowledge that you can't do everything, or that there are things you won't be able to do well? Do you feel a constant need to prove yourself? If so, you might be a perfectionist. Perfectionism most often arises from the core belief that "I am not good enough." A perfectionist will spend most of their time trying to make up for that feeling by striving to be perfect. Self-improvement is often good and healthy, but when we believe that we are failures unless we achieve total perfection, it becomes unhealthy very quickly. Perfectionists get stuck in a constant loop of trying to be perfect, followed by being devastated when they make a mistake, then resolving to try even harder the next time. This is an exhausting and defeating cycle that prevents us from flourishing in life and being free. Yes, it's important to strive to be better and to learn from our mistakes, but this is different from perfectionism. Perfectionism is based on the belief that my worth is dependent on my ability to never make a mistake. Pursuing excellence differs from perfectionism because it is not about proving our worth. Instead, it is about continually working to know ourselves better, strengths and weaknesses, and using that to our advantage when pursuing our authentic purpose.

Fear of vulnerability

Many of us fear being vulnerable with others. We are afraid that if we share our innermost dreams, needs, and thoughts, we might be rejected or belittled for sharing what's truly on our hearts. Perhaps you once chose to share something with another person, and they hurt you by betraying your trust. That is a difficult wound to heal, and it can leave you feeling skittish about sharing with others. It is certainly a risk to share with others because there is always the chance that you might get hurt (even if it's a very small chance). But it is an important part of authentic relationships and an authentic life, because it allows you to create a deeper connection with others. Of course, it is important to discern with whom we share with and what we share with them (that's where prudence comes in!). Still, when we let our fear of being vulnerable rule our lives, we aren't able to truly be our authentic selves because we are keeping important parts of ourselves hidden away.

Entitlement

Life is hard, and it isn't always fair. If you've faced any kind of hardship in your life, you've probably asked God why he made you go through this challenging time. You might have even gotten angry at God or questioned your faith because of these struggles, whether it was a physical ailment, trauma, abuse, financial trouble, relationship challenge, mental health issue, or some other kind of cross. When you've faced hardships or setbacks in life, it can be easy to believe that life owes you good things to make up for your difficulties. If we're not careful, this can turn into a selfish or entitled attitude, where we lose sight of what we are called to do and instead focus on what we want (and these can often be two different things). Instead of seeking healing, looking forward to the future, and feeling hopeful, we get stuck trying to make up for the hardships we endured.

There is also another side of entitlement: When life has been relatively smooth for you, it's easy to fall into the mindset that you are entitled to a continual stream of good things in your life. Or, you might confuse a life of minimal suffering to be a sign that you are doing the right things in life. Then, when you encounter some kind of hardship, that new experience of suffering can be devastating or throw you into a tailspin. It's important to remember that God doesn't owe us anything. Everything given to us is a gift. Saint Thérèse was known to say, "Everything is grace." There is some kind of gift in every experience that God puts in our life. (It is important to note that this is very different from the adage, "Everything happens for a reason." Instead, every experience is some kind of invitation from God to grow closer in our relationship to him, learn something new, conquer some kind of struggle, find healing, and the like.)

Mental health struggles

Your mental and emotional health play a significant role in your ability to live authentically. When you are adequately managing stress and addressing any anxiety, depression, or other mental health struggles you might have, you are better able to make decisions that help you become the person God is calling you to be. On the other hand, when your mental health is suffering, it's much more challenging to know what's best for you. It's hard to know what will help you be more authentically "you" when you aren't really feeling like yourself in the first place. You feel trapped instead of free to live with a sense of purpose. Addressing your mental health is a key component of living an authentic life and pursuing your purpose. It's important to note that needing to address your mental health doesn't put pursuing your purpose on pause. In fact, I would argue that it may be an opportunity to learn more about yourself and what your purpose might be. Don't get stuck thinking that your mental health is preventing you from living a purposeful life — it is 100 percent possible!

Faith struggles

As believers, we must seek answers to the really hard questions in life. Yet God doesn't ask us to naively believe whatever the Church teaches. God created us with reason and free will, and he wants us to exercise both by diving deeper into our faith — including those things we question. Sometimes, though, our quest for answers can lead us into difficulty, fear, and even despair. We become like Peter when he walked on the water: He took his eyes off Jesus, became frightened, and started to drown. When we let fear take over, our faith struggles pull us away from God instead of closer to him. Seeing our purpose in life is much more challenging when we feel far away from God. The good news is he is always waiting to welcome us back, and no struggle we may face can change the reality of his love for us.

People pleasing

A people pleaser is someone who focuses on making others happy at any cost, even to the point of neglecting their own needs. They are so focused on ensuring that others are happy with them, that they put their own well-being on the back burner. People pleasers often feel resentful and unhappy because others take advantage of their "selflessness," or overwhelmed at trying to manage others' emotional responses. In reality, people pleasers are not practicing true selflessness or even truly loving others. Being selfless doesn't mean serving others at the expense of our own well-being and needs, or trying to make other people happy instead of striving for an authentic relationship. Setting appropriate boundaries, and taking care of ourselves while caring for others, ensures that we don't lose sight of our purpose in life.

The reality of sin

We all struggle with the effects of sin. With the exception of Mary, the Mother of God, no human being has ever been immune from the effects of original sin. Sin — especially when we fall into habits or patterns of sin — makes it difficult to discern God's call for our lives. Now, the key isn't to strive to be sinless, but to end the patterns of sin that leave us stuck. It takes courage to pick yourself up again when you sin, ask for forgiveness, and strive to do better next time. And this courage is key to living a meaningful life. Father Jacques Philippe writes in his book *Searching for and Maintaining Peace*, "It is not so much a question of our making superhuman efforts to completely eliminate our imperfections and our sins (that which is, in any case, beyond our reach!), as it is a question of knowing how, as quickly as possible, to recapture our peace when we have fallen into sin or have been troubled by the experience of our imperfections, and to avoid sadness and discouragement." We have to recognize the ways in which our own particular patterns of sin prevent us from living a life of purpose.

Embrace the Challenge

Although these challenges — both external and internal — can make living an intentional and purpose-filled life difficult, they don't make it impossible. The reality is no one has a life completely free from challenges. We need to acknowledge the reality of the challenges we face and empower ourselves to respond to them, rather than buckling under them or wishing them away. When we approach life and its challenges this way, we free ourselves to find God in the present moment and to allow him to show us the purpose he has in mind for us.

As we move forward, we will look at concrete strategies to help you address these external and internal challenges. My hope is that these practical tools will help you feel free to live your life and claim it with purpose.

Yes, this can be challenging work. We have to be willing to do hard work to uncover and identify the often-subtle ways in which external and internal factors are affecting us. These changes won't (and can't) happen overnight. I invite you to approach this as a marathon, not a sprint. Some days are going to be easier than others. You will make mistakes, and you will mess up from time to time, but that's OK. Be patient, keep your eyes on your goal, and resolve to get a little bit better each day. Life is hard and challenging, even when you have a strong sense of purpose. You may have days where you are tempted to just give up, or wonder if the struggle is worth it. I've always found Pope St. John Paul II's words to be encouraging and uplifting in times of uncertainty or struggle. His words can instill hope during difficult times: "Do not be afraid. Do not be satisfied with mediocrity. Put out into the deep and let your nets down for a catch."

Reflection Questions

- Think about someone you know who lives their life in an authentic way. What qualities do they embody?
- How does your definition of success compare or contrast with that of society's?
- How does your faith fit in with living an authentic and purpose-filled life?

Action Items

- Make a list of the external and internal challenges that

affect your life and impede your ability to live freely. Keep this list handy for reference as you work through the rest of this book. As you come across a strategy or practical tip that could help you address one of these challenges, make a note on your list.

- Spend some time brainstorming what being free from the constraints of these external and internal factors would look like. Write down what your life would look like.

- Write down a list of the specific ways in which your core beliefs negatively affect your ability to live with purpose.

9

Play to Your Strengths

Young adults today face a lot of pressure to choose their life's path and be amazing at it. According to our culture — and often our families and mentors as well — a meaningful life is one that includes a prestigious career with a paycheck and lifestyle to match. We're rarely encouraged to stop, take a step back, and ask ourselves, "What am I good at and how can I use this to contribute to the world?" This all-important question easily gets lost as we strive to balance expectations, the realities of needing to support ourselves (and pay off those loans!), and discerning what our gifts and talents are in the first place.

Let's take a look at a hypothetical example of identifying and playing to your strengths:

Tina, in her mid-twenties, was feeling dissatisfied with her career. She had graduated from law school and passed the bar, but she could not find a position that would let her practice the kind of law she was interested in. Instead, her job consisted of reviewing thousands of pages of documents and organizing them — as far away as possible from the vision she'd had of being a lawyer. After about a year, she was so frustrated that she left law completely to take a corporate job in higher education. While that was a refreshing change, she missed being able to offer legal assistance to those who needed it. Her new job still did not provide the sense of meaning and purpose she was searching for. Tina began to ask herself what had initially attracted her to pursuing a career in law and made her think she could excel at it. After many months of self-reflection and conversations with her support network, Tina identified that she enjoyed the challenge of strategizing and finding the best angle for a particular case. She valued being able to help others in need using the law. She also realized that she had a talent for explaining the complexities of the legal system to clients, in a way that few of her law school classmates and colleagues could. She decided to try working again as a lawyer; but this time, she applied exclusively to nonprofits that provided legal aid to people in need, where she would be able to work closely and directly with her clients and see the direct impact of her work. It took a few months, but she finally found a meaningful job that empowered her.

Tina's journey didn't happen overnight. She had to try out jobs that weren't quite right, spend time in honest and vulnerable self-reflection, consult with people she trusted, leave a job and try a new one, and be patient. But the payoff in the end was worth it. She found a job that allowed her to wake up each day excited about her work. The turning point in Tina's story was when she asked herself why she was initially attracted to the legal world, and why she thought she would excel there. By asking herself these questions, she was able to start discerning her unique gifts and talents and how she could use them to the best of her ability.

Like Tina, we need to take the time to identify our strengths and how we can use them best. This will give us greater clarity regarding our purpose in life and the way God is inviting us to live that purpose out. It is important to note that playing to your strengths is not just related to your career. The work that you do is certainly important, but it is not your identity. You are much more than the job you have (or don't have), and your purpose in life extends far beyond the work you do. This means that your talents and gifts can be used not only in your work, but also in every other area of your life. When we use our gifts, we can help others and do good in our communities.

How to Identify Your Strengths

We must identify our unique talents and gifts if we want to fully embrace our life's purpose. This can be a surprisingly difficult task. Most of us can quickly list the things we aren't good at, but naming areas where we excel can be much more challenging. In my first few meetings with new psychotherapy clients, I make it a point to ask them what their strengths are, because this can help us address whatever it is that they are trying to work on in therapy. More often than not, they struggle to come up with even a handful of strengths. And I get it. When we lose sight of our identity as beloved children of God, it's hard to see the good that we can contribute to the world. If we have only received feedback about our faults, we become so hyperfocused on them that our good qualities fade into the background. Sometimes we worry that it's prideful to focus on what we do well. All three of these perspectives are roadblocks that prevent us from freely living with purpose.

If you're not sure where to begin, here are some steps you can take to begin to identify your strengths:

- Make a list of activities, places, experiences, and people that fill you with life and energy.
- Reach out to trusted family, friends, and mentors who know you well and ask them what strengths, gifts, and virtues they see in you. They might be able to identify qualities you have never considered.

- Look for commonalities among your list and the lists others share with you. For example, maybe you'll see a theme of communicating with others through writing, speaking, or even music. Or of helping others feel welcome and at home. Determining these common factors will point you toward the core of who you are and the gifts you have.
- Make a list of ways that you can cultivate and nurture these qualities.
- Brainstorm and create a list of ways you can utilize the qualities you identified. These are the things you want to intentionally do more of in your life.
- Now, make a list of experiences, activities, and places that drain you of your energy and motivation.
- Look for common themes between the items on your list. These things will show you where you probably want to spend less time, attention, and energy.

These steps can help you start to engage in the crucial process of self-reflection to identify the gifts you've been given — whether those are talents, personality traits, characteristics, or virtues — and the best way to use them. Remember, this process takes time if you want to do it well. No matter what anyone tells you, it's OK to take your time to reflect, explore different ways of using your gifts, and even to make mistakes. Stay the course, and you will find the whole process was worth it. In the introduction, I shared my own experience of trial and error as I tried to discern whether being a therapist was the right path for me to use my gifts. It wasn't a smooth ride, and there were many ups and downs, but it was absolutely worth it in the end. Stick with it!

Know Your Limits

As you identify your strengths and gifts, it's also important to know what your limits are. As much as we want to be able to do it all, we simply can't. We're often told, "You can be anything you want!" or "Anything is possible!" when it comes to choosing a career or discerning your path in life. But if I wanted to be a physicist or mathematician, the road would be very bumpy for me, because math is not my strong suit. I've never enjoyed it, and I struggled to understand the concepts in school. When I completed the GRE and received my results, my scores showed that I was twice as strong in verbal skills as I was in math. Those results confirmed for me that I was pursuing a career that I had the skills for. If I had wanted to be a mathematician, could I have done it? Maybe, but it probably would have been a painful and long struggle to get there, and it wouldn't have felt worth it because I wouldn't have enjoyed working in the field (plus, I don't know that anyone would have wanted to hire me!). Life won't always be easy, but we have to recognize when something is unnecessarily challenging. This can be an indication that we're on the wrong path or trying to force ourselves into a mold where we will never fit.

The reality is that we can't do it all, and we don't even *need* to do it all. Tough as this may be to hear, we might not be able to be anything we want to be — especially if what we want to be doesn't line up with the gifts and talents we possess. Identifying our strengths and weaknesses can help illuminate the unique combination of talents and strengths God gave us, so that we can invest more time and energy into growing those talents and doing good in the world in the specific way that we've been called. Instead of focusing on what we think we "should" do or on what society tells us is successful, freedom lies in doing more of what we do well.

We can find freedom in recognizing what we can and can't do — freedom to direct our time, energy, and focus toward the things that we can do, and to avoid wasting our time, energy, and focus on those things beyond our limits. This is an empowering approach and much less frustrating than pushing ourselves beyond our limits. Knowing our limits helps us discern when to push forward and rise to meet a challenge and when to let something go.

A straightforward way to identify your limits is to ask yourself the following questions at the end of every day:

- What are my energy levels (physical and emotional) today?
- Am I making time to take care of myself (physically, mentally, emotionally, relationally, and spiritually)?
- Am I focusing today on those things that I consider part of a meaningful life?
- Do I feel balanced and fulfilled today?

On days when you are feeling drained and unbalanced, take some time to reexamine whether you are working within your limits. Remember that it can take some time to figure out what your limits are, and trial and error is part of that process. Be patient with yourself, give yourself grace when you make mistakes, and don't be afraid to keep trying to figure it out.

Don't Be Afraid to Choose

It can be intimidating to choose a path for your life, whether it be a career, a relationship, or a move. Choosing one path means saying "no" to other potential paths you could have taken. It means closing the door on many possibilities in order to pursue one thing. This can feel like a lot of pressure to choose the "perfect" path. It can be so paralyzing that it seems easier to just not make any decision at all. We sometimes call it "keeping my options open," but in reality, we just don't want to choose. It helps to change our mindset. Instead of seeing the process of choosing as a pass or fail exercise, ask yourself whether what you are choosing is in line with your values. If it is in line with your values, you can't go wrong at least considering this path. Choose things that align with your values, and you have a greater likelihood of being proud of whatever path you do choose. When you have the courage to choose a path, you are freeing yourself to direct your time and energy toward the things that are important to you. Don't be afraid to choose. Just as recognizing your limits can be freeing, so can choosing a path. And remember, you can readjust your approach or decision for most things in life. Yes, there are some exceptions, but most of the time, it's OK to slightly shift or change your mind altogether. I often remind my high school and college clients of this when they are considering majors and careers. It's common for them to worry about making the "right" choice, believing that they have to choose something and stick to it for the rest of their lives, which produces a lot of unnecessary stress and anxiety. Once they realize that it's OK to pick a major and then change their mind or even change careers, the relief is palpable. If high school or college is very much in the rearview mirror, we can all benefit from the reminder that most things in life can be recalibrated and adjusted as needed.

As you make choices in your life, continue to look to your strengths and gifts. God gave them to you specifically for a purpose. He invites you to answer the call to discern how you can best use them for good. Those strengths and gifts hold the key for you to unlock what an authentic life means for you. And God is calling you to use those gifts to share his love with others and ultimately do good in the world. They are so integral to being your truest self and living a purposeful life that when you feel lost in life, you can always return to your strengths and gifts and let them guide you back to living your life with meaning. Play to your God-given strengths, and you can't go wrong!

Reflection Questions

- What messages were present in your family and social circles about what it means to be successful? How were these messages communicated?

- What did people tell you that you were good at when you were younger? What do they say now?
- Is there anything that you'd like to become better at? What are some steps you could take to make that happen?
- What happens when you honestly admit your limitations?

Action Items

- If you haven't already, go through the steps listed in the "How to Identify Your Strengths" section and try to identify at least three strengths.
- List some limits you have, especially any you may have ignored in the past. Write down ways in which it has helped you (or can help you in the future) to recognize each one of these limits.
- Choose one activity that you've been meaning to do for some time and commit to doing it. Keep it small and simple, but commit to seeing it through.

10

Embrace Your Life

You have a purpose that no one else on earth has.

You have a mission to cultivate the gifts God has given to you and to use them for good. No one else has received your unique mission, and God is inviting you to actively participate in his plan by choosing to live authentically every day. This is the specific path he has given you to pursue holiness, do good, and get to Heaven.

And you have what it takes to answer God's call and live out your unique purpose. God has given you what you need to get started. It's up to you to take the time to figure out your call and have the courage to answer it. The concepts and skills we've covered in this book are here to help you along the way. I hope these tools will help you maintain your focus on what really matters in life and will empower you to shape the direction of your life with intention and purpose, as you seek to understand God's plan.

This may seem like a tall order, and living authentically truly is a lifelong process! But don't let that discourage you. We are all on a similar journey, and we each have a choice. We can embrace finding and living out a purposeful life, or we can let ourselves stay stuck and stagnant, afraid to do the work or to make changes that may be necessary. You are giving yourself a jump start simply by beginning to apply the concepts and strategies covered in this book. They're like the necessary clothes, shoes, and gear for a hike. Technically, you could go hiking in formal wear and without the proper equipment, but it would be a much longer and more painful process than it needs to be. As you learn and incorporate the skills from this book, you will get to know yourself better and better, and that in turn will make it easier for you to know how to live a life of purpose in big and small ways. The goal is to develop new habits of thinking and acting and living each day that will empower you to live your life freely and claim it with purpose.

Making changes can be difficult, even when they are changes we want to make. Sometimes pursuing an authentic and meaning-ful life of purpose even requires that we make radical changes. That could look like changing your field of study, switching careers, es-tablishing clear boundaries with a loved one, leaving a relationship, or starting a new one. Stepping away from the familiar is scary and intimidating. Knowing your strengths, practicing self-care, setting boundaries, knowing your priorities, and challenging your expec-tations — these tools will not only make the journey easier, but they will also make the path forward that much clearer. So don't be afraid to answer the call and rise to the occasion. You can abso-lutely do it, and you don't have to do it alone. Use the strategies in this book; lean on the support of your family, friends, and mentors; and invest in your spiritual life — these will all help support you on your journey as you identify your purpose and then embrace it.

I am reminded of a scene from one of my favorite movies, *You've Got Mail* (1998), where the main character, Kathleen, tells her friend that she has decided to close her children's bookstore. She fought to keep it open, but she simply can't keep up with the big box bookstore that opened up in the same part of town. When Kathleen tells her lifelong friend about her decision to close the bookstore, her friend tells her that she is making a courageous decision to try something completely different from what she has known her whole life. The bookstore has been all Kathleen knows. She inherited it from her mother, and it has been her purpose for her entire adult life so far. But making the difficult and heartbreaking decision to close the store gives Kathleen the opportunity to imagine a different life — one still filled with purpose. She uses her knowledge of the children's book publishing industry and her connections with children's book editors to begin writing a children's book. She uses the same gifts and strengths she had before, but now in a slightly different way that provides her with purpose and meaning, even in the midst of the heartbreak of closing her store.

Just like Kathleen, you might be faced with tough or confusing decisions as you seek to actively participate in God's plan for you. No matter where you are in life, you will be faced with endings and beginnings, closed doors and open doors. Whatever you are faced with, whether the path is clear or murky, God is always guiding you and inviting you to give an active "yes" to the life he has planned for you. Often the big picture won't be clear, but even then God will show you the next step when it's time to take it.

I like to call these steps "bread crumbs." Like the story of Hansel and Gretel, God places a bread crumb in front of you, and your job is to keep an eye out for it and pick it up when you see it, trusting that God will give you the next one when the timing is right. These bread crumbs are usually integrated into our daily lives, so it really is important to be watching for them. It could be a conversation with a trusted friend, something that resonates with you on social media, a thought that comes to you in prayer, or a book recommendation (all these things have happened to me). Instead of letting yourself become overwhelmed by trying to figure it all out at once, focus on figuring out the next step and staying in the present moment. The next step God wants us to take is often much smaller and less drastic than we think.

And remember that this process takes time. Lasting change doesn't happen overnight. There's no shortcut, and living our life according to God's plan is a journey we'll be on every day. It's not always a glamorous journey, either. It takes dedication, hard work, and making the best choice instead of the easiest one. We will all make mistakes along the way. This is not a sign of failure, but simply our reality as imperfect human beings. Even then, we can choose to learn from our mistakes and keep going, trying to do just a little bit better every day than we did the day before.

So where do you go from here? Commit to taking action. If you haven't already, I recommend that you complete the reflection questions and action items at the end of each chapter in this book. Pick one concept or strategy to start with so that you don't take on too much and become discouraged. When it comes to making any big life changes, I like to use the analogy of training for a marathon. If you try to go from barely working out to running a marathon, you will injure yourself because you didn't train properly before-hand. You need to follow a training program instead, starting out with shorter runs before gradually progressing to longer ones. The same approach applies to incorporating a new skill or strategy into the daily fabric of your life. By starting small and building up your "muscle," you prepare yourself to be successful in the long term. So pick one strategy (like setting boundaries, for example) and choose one way in which you'd like to practice it in your daily life. Once you feel like you have a relatively good handle on that strategy, add in another. Build up your strength over time, and you will feel confident about your ability to follow a path of meaning and purpose.

The concepts and skills shared in this book are your tools for the journey, but where you are going is up to you. You have an exciting life ahead of you, and you are invited to do great things with the strengths and gifts God has given you. It's an adventure — and one that you are now prepared to begin! Embrace your purpose with courage and excitement. Dare to imagine a life full of purpose and authenticity.

Questions for Group Discussion

Introduction
- What is the definition of a successful life in popular culture? Do you agree or disagree with this definition?
- Why do you think so many young adults feel anxious about the future or adrift?
- What does living a purposeful life look like to you?

Chapter 1 – Who Are You?
- Why do you think we struggle with truly believing that our worth comes from God's love for us?
- What are some of the false friends that you see many people struggling with in your season of life?
- How does society impact the power these false friends have in our stories?

Chapter 2 — Expectations

- What are some ways society sets up unrealistic or unhealthy expectations for us?
- Are there positive changes happening in society to address these unhealthy or unrealistic standards (aside from the example given in this chapter)?
- Think of a character from a movie or book who has unrealistic expectations. How do these expectations inform the ways he or she thinks, feels, and acts during the course of the story? What is the result?

Chapter 3 — Priorities

- Why do you think priorities are so difficult to keep?
- Name someone you admire for living their life in accordance with their values and priorities. Explain.
- What does society tell us about values and priorities? Do you agree or disagree?

Chapter 4 — Decisions, Decisions, Decisions

- Why do we tend to be wary of our emotions?
- How do the results of the Jam Experiment apply to our everyday life? How have we been negatively impacted by having too many choices?
- What are some helpful strategies you've learned or developed for making decisions?

Chapter 5 — Boundaries

- Why do you think many of us struggle with people-pleasing behaviors?
- What's an example from a book or movie that shows the importance of having healthy boundaries?
- Can you identify a story from Scripture that shows a healthy boundary being set?

Chapter 6 — Self-Care Comes First
- Why do you think is it so challenging to manage stress in our lives?
- Why do you think authentic self-care is often misunderstood and confused with the "treat yourself" mentality?
- Why do you think we all experience the disconnect between our head and heart?

Chapter 7 — Owning Your Worth
- What are some of the messages that we receive from society and culture about our worth?
- What can we do as Catholics and Christians to help spread the message in our daily lives of God's unconditional love for us?
- What individuals (saints, popular figures in history) do you admire, who clearly lived their lives out of the conviction of God's love for each and every one of us?

Chapter 8 — Real-World Challenges to Living Authentically
- Why do you think we have trouble being vulnerable with others, even those we are close to?
- How do you think perfectionism is different from pursuing excellence?
- How do you think having a religious belief influences our beliefs about what it means to live a meaningful life?

Chapter 9 — Play to Your Strengths
- Why do you think it's so difficult for many people to talk about their positive qualities and strengths?
- Did you receive the message "You can be anything

you want to be" when you were younger? What do
you think is true or untrue about this statement?

- Why is it so difficult to commit? Is it harder in some
  areas of life than others? If yes, what are those areas?

Chapter 10 — Embrace Your Life

- What do you think about the concept of God placing
  "bread crumbs" in your life? When was a time when
  you noticed a bread crumb being placed in your path?
- Why do you think lasting change most often doesn't
  happen overnight? Why do you think we prefer in-
  stant change?
- How is your perspective on living a purposeful life
  different from when you started reading this book?
- What is a "courageous decision" that you are facing
  like Kathleen Kelly from *You've Got Mail*?

Acknowledgments

This book would not be possible without the support of so many people! When I set out to compile a list of the skills I wish we all were taught in school, I was incredibly fortunate to have a wealth of resources and incredibly helpful people to lean on for both assistance and inspiration throughout this whole process.

As always, I am grateful for the support and love of my husband and my family. They are always encouraging and my biggest cheerleaders. Writing a book and seeing it published is a surprisingly long process that is slow at times and intense at others, and so it is incredibly valuable to have a strong support system that is constant throughout the whole process.

I was fortunate to have not one but two editors help me with this book. Mary Beth Giltner helped me talk through my many, many, many topic ideas and guided me through the process of narrowing my focus and coming up with the most helpful tone and content. I am also grateful to my other wonderful editor, Rebecca Martin, who took over for Mary Beth and helped my book cross the finish line. You have both made this book so much better than

I could have ever done on my own. It is a true privilege to work with you. Additionally, the entire team at OSV is made up of the most wonderful people. I always feel supported and cared for by everyone there.

I am also thankful for the friends, fellow authors, and unofficial mentors whose ideas and writings helped me to learn the skills I wrote about in this book. I am so grateful for their expertise and that they chose to share their ideas with the world. They provided the education I was searching for on all of these topics.

I am also humbled and honored to be able to work with my clients. They are some of the strongest, most resilient, and wisest people that I know. Though I hope I have helped them in some way, I know that I have learned so much from their examples. Thank you for trusting me as part of your healing journey.

God is good!

About the Author

Julia Marie Hogan Werner, MS, LCPC, is a counselor in Chicago and owner of Vita Optimum Counseling & Consulting, LLC, a private practice that specializes in faith-based psychotherapy. She also leads workshops and writes on topics related to self-care, authentic living, relationships, and mental health. Her book, *It's OK to Start with You*, is all about the power of authentic self-care from a Catholic/Christian perspective. She is passionate about empowering individuals to be their most authentic selves. You can find more of her writing online at juliamariehogan.com.